D1452060

Church and Community

J. H. BETTEY # Church & Community

The Parish Church in English Life

BARNES & NOBLE
BOOKS
10 East 53d St., New York 10022
(a division of Harper & Row Publishers, Inc.)

Library of Congress Cataloging in Publication Data
Bettey, J H
　Church & community
　Bibliography: p. 138
　Includes index.
　1. Parishes—England.　2. England—Religious
life and customs.　3. England—Church history.
I. Title.
BR744.B443　　　274.1　　　79–14739
ISBN 0–06–490381–8

Published in the U.S.A. 1979 by
HARPER & ROW PUBLISHERS, INC.
BARNES & NOBLE IMPORT DIVISION
ISBN 0–06–490381–8
Printed and bound in Great Britain

Contents

List of Illustrations

List of Illustrations

Preface

For many centuries the parish churches of England were the social as well as the religious centres of the communities which they served; the churches were by far the largest, and often the only public buildings, and the church provided the focal point for almost all village activities—charitable, educational and recreational—as well as religious. The purpose of the following chapters is to describe the different ways in which the church buildings and their surroundings have been used by local communities, the attitude of parishioners towards their parish churches and the vital part which the churches have played in the secular as well as the religious life of the communities. The parish churches to be described will be mainly those village churches which served the rural communities in which, until the last two centuries, most of the people of England lived.

It is not intended to add to the many studies which have already been made of the architecture of parish churches, nor to the existing books on the craftsmanship in stone, wood, glass and metal to be found within them, but to discuss the evidence which survives for the use of the buildings, their role in the life of parishes, and the ways in which this changed over the centuries.

1. Parish churches and church services during the Middle Ages

By the time of the Norman Conquest or soon afterwards the parochial system was firmly established in most parts of England; and parishes had replaced the earlier ecclesiastical organisation based on scattered 'minster' churches. These minsters were originally the missionary centres from which priests made preaching journeys into the surrounding pagan countryside, to teach, to celebrate mass and to baptise converts. The process whereby such minsters were established was a slow one, and it was not until three or four centuries after St Augustine's arrival in Canterbury in 597 that most of the country came within the sphere of influence of a minster church and its clergy. The memory of several former minsters survives in Dorset place-names such as Beaminster, Yetminster, Charminster, Wimborne Minster and Iwerne Minster. In Devon the place-name evidence suggests that there were minsters at Axminster and Exminster, while documentary evidence confirms that there were also early minsters at Crediton, Braunton, Plymton and Coryton. Place-names show that minsters existed in Somerset at Pitminster, Ilminster, Bedminster and Godminster, while early charters provide evidence for minsters at Wells, Taunton and East Pennard, and King Alfred's will mentions the minster at Cheddar. In the region around Canterbury minsters were established at Reculver, Minster-in-Thanet, Dover, Folkestone, Lyminge, Minster-in-Sheppey and Hoo; and there is documentary evidence for the founding of minsters during the seventh and eighth centuries at several places in England, including Breedon-on-the-Hill in Leicestershire, Brixworth in Northamptonshire, Corbridge in Northumberland, Monkwearmouth in County Durham and many others. In some churches also, the survival of substantial remains of the pre-Conquest architecture provides evidence that these were originally minster churches. Examples are to be found all over England, including Hexham, Ripon, York, Escomb in county Durham and Deerhurst in Gloucestershire. Among the finest survivals of early minsters is the church at Brixworth in Northamptonshire. Both Brixworth and Breedon-on-the-Hill in Leicestershire were founded in the later seventh century as minsters by the monastery at Peterborough, and were intended to serve as centres for the conversion of the surrounding areas. The church which provides perhaps the most striking evidence of its origin as a missionary centre and which also reveals something of the fervour and enthusiasm of the early Christian preachers is Breamore in Hampshire; a tenth-century arch inside the church has deeply cut above it the Anglo-Saxon inscription HER SWVTELAD SEO GECWYDRAEDNES DE—'In this place the Word is revealed unto thee'. Above the entrance to the church at Breamore is the Anglo-Saxon rood, the figure of the crucified Christ, with body twisted in the agony of crucifixion, still a powerfully moving work of art in spite of the mutilation which it received at the hands of reformers during the sixteenth century. At first the places regularly visited by the missionary priests from the minsters were marked by crosses and these survive, either entire or in fragments, in many places, especially in Cornwall, but many of the crosses were soon replaced by small churches, and gradually these became established as parish churches with their own resident priest. More than 350 early stone crosses survive in Cornwall, and many are beside or near the sites of later churches. Thus for example the little Cornish church of St Piran in the Sands which dates from the sixth century and is the earliest surviving church in south-west England, has beside it an early stone cross, and near many other west-country churches there are crosses or the remains of crosses which pre-date the churches themselves. The minster system was only suited to the missionary stage of church life, and the parochial system slowly evolved to meet the need for a closer pastoral ministry.

Many of the earliest churches were of wood, but the evidence of their existence has vanished during successive rebuildings and enlargements in stone, or could only now be revealed by archaeological excavation beneath the existing churches. A few documentary references to these early wooden churches survive. The Venerable Bede writing in the eighth century commented that many churches were built '*more Scottorum non de lapida*' (after the manner of the Scots not of stone); Bede also records that when St Aldhelm, the first bishop of Sherborne, died in 709 while he was conducting a visitation of his diocese, he was taken into the church at Doulting in Somerset where there was 'a wooden church into which as he was breathing his last he ordered that he should be carried'. An early life of St Dunstan, the tenth-century Abbot of Glastonbury who became Archbishop of Canterbury, described how when he came to Glastonbury there was a wooden church there and that while he was Abbot parts of the wooden structure were rebuilt in stone. At Mayfield St Dunstan found the church consisted merely of a construction of the boughs of trees over the altar, and he was able to align it more accurately to the east simply by pushing at it with his shoulder. An example of an early church constructed of roughly-hewn, split tree trunks survives at Greenstead in Essex, and excavation of the site of St Michael's church Thetford, (Norfolk) has shown that the earliest church on the site was a timber building and that during the eleventh century it was replaced by a stone structure of identical plan and proportions; in the twelfth century the church was enlarged by extending the nave. It has also been suggested that a possible reason why the walls of surviving Saxon churches such as those at Deerhurst in Gloucestershire, Brixworth in Northamptonshire, Jarrow in County Durham, Bradford-on-Avon in Wiltshire, and many others are so high may be because they were originally timber structures which would have been easier to build at such heights, and that when they were gradually rebuilt in stone the same height and roof-line was maintained.

Once it was established, each parish became a separate ecclesiastical unit, with clearly defined boundaries, whose inhabitants owed allegiance to their own parish church and were forbidden to worship at any other. The majority of the rural parishes throughout the Middle Ages contained communities of not more than 50 or 60 households or some 250–300 souls; and at the heart of each of these little rural communities was the parish church. Originally many of these churches owed their existence to the local lord of the manor, who built a church to serve the needs of the tenants on his estate and who retained the advowson or right to appoint the parish priest. Throughout the Middle Ages, however, most parish churches were subject to successive rebuildings, alterations and enlargements, reflecting both increases in population and a growth in the prosperity of the parish community, so that by the fifteenth century few retained more than a vestige of the original church which once occupied the same site. The extent of the changes and alterations which many parish churches have undergone can generally only be fully revealed by archaeological excavation, and opportunities for such detailed investigation are rare. Excavations carried out on the site of the church of St Paul-in-the-Bail in Lincoln have shown that there have been at least 17 different phases of church building, rebuilding, enlargement and alteration to the structure during the period from the seventh century to the present. This excavation reminds us that often the existing church buildings, even those of medieval date, are not by any means the earliest churches in that place, and that many outwardly late and unpromising churches in fact occupy the sites and incorporate material from much earlier buildings. Archaeological excavation in the church at Rivenhall in Essex, which was formerly thought to be a Victorian re-building, has revealed a Roman building under part of the chancel and has shown that part of the structure of the church is of Saxon origin. Similarly, excavation in the church at Hadstock, Essex, has shown that the eleventh-century church there incorporates several periods of Saxon work within a very complicated structure. The church of St Martin at the site of the deserted village of Wharram Percy in the East Riding of Yorkshire has been shown to have undergone some 12 stages of building-development from the late eighth century to the nineteenth century.

For most of our knowledge of church life and of the attitude of parishioners towards their parish churches during the early centuries of Christianity we have to depend very heavily upon the evidence of the buildings themselves, their siting, structure and decoration, for there are few local documentary sources of information on services or parish life. The siting of parish churches is often of very great interest in its own right, since the earliest churches were frequently built in places which already had very long traditions of pre-Christian religious worship. It is also well known that the parish church frequently continued to occupy its original site even after the village community had moved to another part of the parish, and many of the isolated churches of the south-west, such as Holcombe in Somerset, Cameley in Avon, Kempley in Gloucestershire, St Enoder in Cornwall and many others, provide evidence of the former location of such villages. In places it can also be observed that the village was in existence before the coming of the church. A good example of this is at Ashmore, high up on the chalk downs of Cranborne Chase on the Wiltshire-Dorset border, where the village clusters tightly around its only water supply and the feature from which it takes its name, a large circular pond, the 'Ash-mere'. At Ashmore, which was in existence long before the coming of Christianity, the central area all around the pond is occupied by houses, and when in the Saxon period a parish church was required, it had to be placed on the only available site which is some way outside the central nucleus of the village. At Knowlton, also on Cranborne Chase, the church, which is now a ruin but which was in regular use until the eighteenth century, was built on a site away from the village for another reason. Knowlton church was constructed in the centre of a notable neolithic 'henge' or ritual earthwork and it is surrounded by the circular bank and ditch.

PRE-CHRISTIAN INFLUENCES

Many other parish churches also occupy pre-Christian religious sites. For example, at Moreton in south-east Dorset the church stands on a prehistoric burial mound; at Brentor (Devon) the church is within an earthwork on top of the high tor; at Oldbury-on-Severn in Avon the church is away from the village and within the ramparts of a prehistoric earthwork; at both Avebury (Wilts) and Stanton Drew (Avon) the parish churches stand within or beside the great prehistoric stone circles; while at Maiden Bradley (Wilts) the church is situated on or beside a Roman burial ground. A good example of the use by the Christian church of a former pagan site is at Rudston in Yorkshire. Here the church stands in a circular churchyard which at once suggests a pre-Christian religious site, and beside the church stands one of the largest stone monoliths in the country together with a smaller, triangular standing stone. Fimber church in Yorkshire stands upon a Bronze Age barrow, and Edlesborough in Buckinghamshire is prominently situated upon a mound which was probably a barrow, and was certainly a site of pagan significance, while the church at West Wycombe in the same county stands inside an Iron Age earthwork. Ludlow parish church is by the site of a large barrow or prehistoric burial mound which had to be removed in 1199 when the church was enlarged. Recent work on place-name derivations has revealed that the churches at both Harrow in Middlesex and Wednesbury in Staffordshire are on the sites of former pagan shrines. The Cornish churches of St Clement, St Kew and Lewannick have inscribed stones which may well be pre-Christian in origin, and the church at St Issey was originally known as Egloscruk—i.e. the church on the burial mound— and no doubt occupies a site of some pre-Christian religious significance.

Many churches also contain carvings and symbols of pagan religious and fertility cults. Early Christian leaders were reluctant to impose too heavy a conflict of loyalties upon new converts, and thus pagan sites were turned into Christian churches and associated with a saint rather than with a heathen god, the pagan festivals were incorporated into the Christian year, and pagan symbols continued to be carved on churches. Springs and wells which had been associated with pagan worship were assimilated into the Christian church and became holy wells, so that for example in Cornwall there are more than 100 holy wells, many of them bearing the names of local saints and often also being associated with various legends of the saints. There can be no doubt that this assimilation was a conscious policy on the part of the early Church in England. In a letter written in 601 AD by Pope Gregory the Great to the Abbot Mellitus, one of the early missionaries who accompanied St Augustine to Canterbury, the Pope declared that he had given much thought to the conversion of the English and advised that the pagan temples should not be destroyed, but rather purified with holy water and that Christian altars should be set up within them instead of idols:

Destroy the idols; purify the buildings with holy water; set relics there; and let them become temples of the true God. So the people will have no need to change their places of concourse, and where of old they were wont to sacrifice cattle to demons, thither let them continue to resort on the day of the saint to whom the church is dedicated, and slay their beasts no longer as a sacrifice, but for a social meal in honour of Him whom they now worship.

Thus in surroundings which already had powerful and familiar religious associations the people would be won more easily to the new faith. The pope ended his letter to Mellitus with the astute observation that if a man wishes to climb he should do so by steps and not by leaps. An eighth-century life of St Samson records how when on a missionary journey through Cornwall, the saint smashed the idol in a pagan temple and replaced it by a stone which he marked with a cross, and it seems likely that similar processes whereby an originally pagan shrine became a Christian church occurred in many other places, although only rarely does documentary or archaeological evidence exist to confirm this. It remains a matter for speculation why from the earliest surviving Saxon stone churches to the large, elegant and sophisticated structures of the later Middle Ages it seemed proper to the builders to include a mass of pagan symbols and a whole array of monsters, grotesques, obscene persons and mythical creatures. But there can be no doubt of the strength of the tradition, and examples are to be found both inside and outside churches throughout the country. The claim to abundant supernatural power in the fight against the pagan demons was an essential element in the teaching of the early missionary church in England, and no doubt the missionaries as well as later churchmen did not fail to stress the superiority of Christian prayers to heathen charms, either in their sermons or in the carvings on their churches. In spite of all the efforts of puritan reformers and Victorian

1. *Knowlton Church, Dorset* The church, which fell into ruin in the eighteenth century, is situated away from the village and in the middle of a prehistoric 'henge' or ritual enclosure.

2. *Male Fertility Figure, Abson, Avon* This blatantly masculine figure is on the east wall of the chancel, and probably dates from the twelfth century.

3. *Green Man, Crowcombe, Somerset* The Green Man was popular with west-country carvers throughout the Middle Ages; this example is on a bench-end dated 1534.

restorers, the survival into the twentieth century of so many pagan and frankly sensual subjects as well as pre-Christian religious symbols on numerous parish churches bears striking witness to the continuing influence of older cults upon medieval parishioners and church builders, and to the persistence of the idea of a conflict between good and evil which so powerfully occupied the minds of church carvers.

Roman altar-stones are to be found built into the churches at Compton Dando (Avon), where there is an altar to Jupiter, and at Tockenham (Wilts) where there is an altar to Aesculapius. There are Roman altars in the church porch at Caerwent (Monmouthshire) and in the crypt at Hexham (Northumberland), and many other churches have Roman figures or make use of Roman building materials, including Cirencester, Daglingworth and Churcham in Gloucestershire, Mildenhall in Wiltshire and Whitechurch Canonicorum in Dorset, Corbridge in Northumberland and Bradwell-on-Sea in Essex. There are Roman milestones in the churches or churchyards at St Hilary, Breage and Tintagel in Cornwall, a stoup in the church at Michaelchurch (Herefordshire) has been cut from a Roman altar, and similarly a re-cut Roman altar serves as a font at Lund (Lancashire). Carvings of the Green Man, the pre-Christian symbol of vegetable fertility, a figure surrounded by foliage and often with leaves emerging from mouth, nose and ears, are to be found both inside and on the exterior of countless churches from an early town church like St John's, Devizes (Wiltshire) to a late medieval church like St Mary Redcliffe (Bristol) or Bishops Lydiard (Somerset). The Green Man peers down through the foliage on many roof bosses, including a well-known example in the cloisters of Norwich cathedral and another at Pershore; he is also constantly to be found among the carvings in smaller village churches such as Kilpeck (Herefordshire), Longdon (Staffordshire), Great Durnford (Wiltshire) and innumerable others. Not infrequently the pagan Green Man is to be found incorporated into Christian carvings, as at East Brent (Somerset), where on the western face of the late medieval tower a series of carvings depicting the Trinity and the Blessed Virgin rest firmly on the figure of the Green Man.

Another notable pre-Christian figure is to be found carved on part of a ninth-century Saxon cross-shaft in the church of Codford St Peter (Wiltshire). This shows an elegant male figure with head thrown back, holding a branch of foliage in one hand and executing a stylised dance. This remarkably powerful and lively carving is probably the representation of a spring dance or pagan festival to mark the end of winter, and the fact that it appears on a cross shaft is further evidence of the mixture of pagan and sacred emblems which are so frequently to be found together in churches.

Even more remarkable survivals are the male and female fertility symbols which are still to be found on a few churches; these no doubt are the chance survivors of many other similar carvings which have over the years fallen victim to those who have regarded them as obscene or un-Christian. Examples of the female fertility figure known as a 'Sheila-na-Gig', which consists of a grotesque female carving with exaggerated sexual organs, are to be found at Oaksey on the borders of Wiltshire and Gloucestershire, at Whittlesford in Cambridgeshire, and on the little Norman church at Kilpeck in Herefordshire. Male fertility figures, again with greatly exaggerated sexual organs, still survive at Abson (Avon) and Haresfield (Glos.), although the latter is very badly weathered and perhaps deliberately defaced. The most notable male fertility figure is not on a church at all, but cut in the chalk hillside above the parish church and the site of the pre-Conquest Benedictine Abbey at Cerne Abbas. The survival of the Cerne Giant in such a position is one of the great mysteries of west-country history and archaeology; and to make the puzzle even more tantalizing there is not a single documentary reference to the Giant before the mid-eighteenth century, even though a large number of documents survive relating to the landscape and history of Cerne Abbas.

Many churches also contain carvings from the Saxon and Norman periods depicting beasts, dragons, monsters, or originally pagan symbolism such as the tree of life, astrological signs or the frantic patterns of inter-laced scrolls and knots. The persistence of these symbols is a remarkable tribute to the tenacity of the ancient beliefs and superstitions and to the sub-culture of witchcraft, magic, fertility cults and the acceptance of the reality of the presence of the forces of evil which remained current throughout the Middle Ages. Even on bench-ends put in to churches as late as the sixteenth century the Green Man, the Tree of Life, the signs of the Zodiac and the pagan gods continue to appear, as well as a whole assortment of demons, devils, grotesques, monsters and obscene creatures.

It is clear from the evidence of the buildings themselves, that powerful among the attitudes of parishioners towards their churches during these early centuries of Christianity was their feeling, which has already been mentioned, of the conflict between the forces of good and evil, and the necessity for the protection of the church and its sacraments if the assaults of the devil and his hosts upon the individual soul were to be resisted.

This sense of the protection afforded by the church to the otherwise helpless soul, and of the incessant conflict with the powers of darkness, is seen in the many Norman carvings of the battle between St Michael and the devil or the dragon: as for example on the north wall of Stoke-sub-Hamdon in south Somerset or on the notable Norman font at Luppitt in Devon; or the conflicts between angels and dragons carved on the Norman tympana at Ruardean in the Forest of Dean, at Hoveringham in Nottinghamshire and at Moreton Valence near Gloucester; or in the conflict between the virtues and their contrary vices depicted on the Norman fonts of Stanton Fitzwarren in Wiltshire or Southrop in Gloucestershire. At Stanton Fitzwarren, for example, the virtues—*Largitas, Humilitas, Pietas, Misericordia, Modestia, Temperencia, Paciencia* and *Pudicicia*—are shown trampling upon their corresponding vices—*Avaricia, Superbia, Discordia, Invidia, Ebrietas, Luxuria, Ira* and *Libido*. At Southrop the figures of the vices each have their names carved backwards or in 'mirror' writing on the panels as a further indication of their wickedness, while around the top of the font, above the conflict, are depicted the heavenly mansions to which the soul may aspire by holding fast to the virtues through the help of the church while eschewing the vices and all the works of the devil.

The same idea of conflict and of the essential protection afforded by the church and its sacraments is seen in the Latin inscription around the rim of the ornate Norman font at Lullington, near Frome in Somerset, which reads: *Hoc fontis sacro pereunt delicta lavacro* ('In this holy font sins perish and are washed away'). During the later medieval centuries the same sort of imagery designed to convey an identical message occurs in the paintings with which the walls of many churches were so lavishly decorated, and in the stained-glass windows. The great 'Doom' or Last Judgement was depicted over the chancel arch, and survives at Wenhaston in Suffolk, Chaldon in Surrey, Clayton in Sussex and St Thomas' Salisbury, as well as in the powerful west window at Fairford in Gloucestershire; while the legends of St Christopher, St George, the Three Living Knights meeting their three dead counterparts and many other such stories were depicted on the walls of countless churches and survive, for example, at Pickering in Yorkshire, Gussage St Andrew in Dorset, Ditcheat in Somerset, Witley in Surrey, Kempley in Gloucestershire, Raunds in Northamptonshire, Pickworth in Lincolnshire and at Breage in Cornwall, and in countless other churches throughout the country.

THE SERVICES IN THE MEDIEVAL PARISH CHURCH

When we turn to consider what the services of the medieval parish church were like and how the parishioners conducted themselves in church, whether they attended all the services, how far they understood them and what their attitude towards the church and its sacraments was, we have very little firm evidence to guide us until the end of the Middle Ages, when churchwardens' accounts and other documentary sources become available. Perhaps the most important single piece of evidence that parishioners were closely and actively involved in the life of the church lies in the fact that almost all churches were rebuilt or enlarged at least once during the Middle Ages, that most had additional chapels and aisles added or a western tower built, and that almost all were constantly redecorated and adorned. As will be shown later, most of the money for this highly expensive work came from the parishioners themselves, and whatever their motives for contributing, men do not give large sums of money to causes in which they are not vitally interested.

As for the services, there were generally three services for the laity on Sundays and Holy Days, Mattins followed by Mass during the morning, and Evensong during the afternoon. Langland in *Piers Plowman* wrote that 'Upon Sundays to cease, God's service to hear, Both mattins and mass, and, after meat, in churches To hear their evensong every man ought.' This was the ideal, and parishioners should have attended all three services in their own parish churches, but many contented themselves with coming to Mass, and used the afternoons for recreation or merry-making. Mass was said daily by the parish priest, but in rural parishes few of the laity were able to attend these services. In the larger churches and in the towns there were often many more daily services, especially in the later Middle Ages when the number of clergy increased tremendously. As early as 1377 the poll-tax returns reveal that there were, for example, 1,315 clergy in Devon, or roughly one priest to every 55 people in the county, and the number of clergy was to increase considerably during the fifteenth century. A study of the clergy in Wiltshire during the century before the Reformation has shown that even the smallest and most remote churches had at least one priest, and that in most places there were two or more stipendiary chaplains and chantry priests in addition to the rector or vicar. A visitation of Sonning in Berkshire in 1220 revealed that there were seven curates or chaplains there besides the Vicar, and at Snaith in Yorkshire in 1275 there were six chaplains as well as the vicar. Such examples might be multiplied many times, and the number of clergy, far from diminishing, increased substantially during the later Middle Ages. It is unlikely that the services of the church were particularly attractive or interesting for the average medieval congregation. The service was in Latin and was often spoken by a priest whose knowledge of that language may have been only slightly greater than that of his congregation; there was little opportunity for the laity to participate, for there were no hymns in the early Middle Ages and only occasionally a sermon, and until the late fourteenth century there were no seats in the nave, so the congregation had either to kneel or stand. The churches were also unheated, and must have been very cold and uncomfortable during the winter. The laity were concerned only to hear the Mass, for they normally only received the sacrament once a year at Easter, after making their confessions and receiving absolution. In such circumstances it is not surprising that there were many complaints about inattention, talking and irreverent behaviour by the laity. John Myrc, a canon of Lilleshall in Shropshire who wrote a manual of *Instructions for Parish Priests* in 1400, was at pains to emphasize the importance of reverent behaviour in church, though probably few congregations reached the standard which he set. Myrc instructs the parish priest that he should teach his people to behave reverently and to avoid talking and 'ydel speeche'; they should also be taught to:

> . . . put away alle vantye
> And say their Pater Noster and their Ave,
> Nor none in churche stonde schall,
> Nor leane to pylar nor to wall,
> But fayre on knees they schalle them sette,
> Kneeling down up on the flatte,
> And pray to God wyth hearte meeke,
> To give them grace and mercy eke.

The people are also to be instructed to stand up for the reading of the Gospel, and, above all, to kneel reverently when the bell was rung to mark the consecration of the Host, the supreme moment of the Mass. We can, however, only speculate as to how many congregations in parish churches conformed to Myrc's ideal.

As far as the beliefs of the laity are concerned, all the evidence points to the fact that these consisted of an extremely simple and total acceptance of a few basic concepts. The paintings on the walls of medieval churches, the stained glass and the sermons of medieval preachers all tended to emphasize the inevitability of judgement and of a destiny that consisted of either perpetual bliss or of constant and eternal torment; to achieve the one and avoid the other could only be done through the prayers of the Church and the intercession of the saints, and above all through the sacrifice of Christ on the Cross and the re-enactment of this sacrifice through the Mass. Belief in the Real Presence of Christ in the Mass was central to all else. Myrc puts this in its plainest terms when he exhorts the parish priest to emphasise the importance of the Mass:

> Teche them thenne with goode intent
> To believe on that sacrament;
> That they receive in forme of bred
> It ys goddes body that suffered ded
> Upon the holy roode tree
> To buye our synnes and make us free.

The regular round of festivals with their processions and other ceremonies served to emphasise this simple, direct message; ashes sprinkled on the congregation on Ash Wednesday in token of penitence, candles carried in procession at Candlemas, Rogationtide processions and the ceremonies of Christmas, Easter and Lammas, all reinforced the essential basis of medieval beliefs. The popular devotion to the Sacrament and to the doctrine of Transubstantiation was greatly strengthened by the growth in popularity of the feast of Corpus Christi, which, from the thirteenth century onwards became one of the most popular of all Christian festivals, and, since it fell in the summer was very suitable for celebrating by outdoor processions when the sacred Host was carried around the parish, and by other festivities. The churchwardens' accounts of Yeovil for 1458 give some indication of the ritual accompanying these processions; the parish bought 2½ yards of linen to make banners together with wooden poles for the banners; they also purchased a cloth to carry over the Host, while one penny was spent on refreshment for the ringers 'for ringing at the Feast of Corpus Christi while the procession went round the town.' At nearby Tintinhull in 1433 the churchwardens purchased a latten pyx for carrying the sacrament in procession on Corpus Christi day. Shrines containing relics of the saints were also the object of great devotion as well as an important source of income from offerings. The complete stone shrine of St Wite survives as an altar at Whitechurch Canonicorum in west Dorset, and is said to have been the scene of many miraculous cures and to have been venerated for long after the Reformation. The shrine containing the relics of St Piran which was kept in the church of Perranzabuloe, Cornwall, was a popular place of pilgrimage throughout the Middle Ages, and the relics were also carried by the parishioners in procession to various places in the vicinity in order to attract the offerings of the faithful. An inventory made in 1281 of the goods of the church of St Piran mentions the head of the Saint and other relics including his staff and copper bell, as well as teeth of St Brendan and St Martin. The cult of relics was of course exceedingly open to abuse and superstition, and to the deception of the simple-minded. The profits to be made from offerings which the faithful made to relics led to a ridiculous proliferation of such things, and to a situation which provoked the angry protest of reformers in the sixteenth century. Charing church in Kent, for example, made great profit from displaying the actual block upon which John the Baptist had been beheaded; St Edmund's, Salisbury, possessed a hand of the saint; St Denis', Stanford-in-the-Vale (Berkshire) venerated a single bone of the saint's body; and there were countless similar examples. Thomas Cromwell's commissioners who visited churches and monasteries during the 1530s poured vast contempt on such cults. One of them, Richard Layton, writing from Bristol described how in one church he had found what was claimed as the actual stone manger in which Jesus had been laid in Bethlehem, and wrote 'belyke there is in Bethlehem plentie of stones and sum quarrie, and makith there mangers of stone'. Another commissioner wrote to Cromwell from Bury St Edmunds that he had found 'the coals that St Lawrence was toasted withal, the parings of St Edmund's nails, St Thomas of Canterbury's penknife and his boots, and divers skills for the headache, pieces of the holy cross able to (enough to) make a holy cross of . . . .' and many others. At Bangor in north Wales another of Cromwell's servants found in one church preserved as a relic the ear of Malchus which St Peter had struck off in the Garden of Gethsemane.

Processions, both inside the church and around parts of the village or parish, were always popular, and the bench-ends at Trull near Taunton show a complete procession including a crossbearer, taper-bearer, a man with an open book, another carrying a shrine and a priest in a cope. The churchwardens at Yatton (Avon) in 1499 spent the enormous sum of £18 on a cross to be carried at the head of processions, while at Croscombe (Somerset) during the fifteenth century the main source of income for the churchwardens was from collections made each year while processions went round the parish. To some extent the ceremonial of processions and the ritual accompanying the mass and other services supplied the place of congregational participation. Another popular ritual was associated with the annual enactment of the Easter Sepulchre, when the Sacred Host was taken from the altar on Good Friday and laid in a specially prepared tomb, generally situated on the north side of the chancel. Here it was watched over by men of the parish during Good Friday and Holy Saturday until at Mass on Easter Day the Host was ceremonially restored to the high altar with the dramatic *Quem Quaeritis* ceremony. This ceremony, symbolising the death, burial and resurrection of Christ, was very popular and was universally enacted in parish churches. A few of the Easter Sepulchres survive in country churches, for example the richly carved sepulchres at Hawton in Nottinghamshire and Heckington in Lincolnshire, or at Tarrant Hinton in Dorset where the elaborate sepulchre is inscribed with the words of the angel to the women at the empty tomb on the first Easter Day *Venire et Videte Locum Ubi Positus Erat Dominus* ('Come and see the place where the Lord lay'). There are also many documentary references to the ceremony of the Easter sepulchre. For example, William Canynge, the fifteenth-century Bristol merchant, gave to St Mary Redcliffe an Easter Sepulchre which included a representation of 'Heaven made of timber and stained clothes', as well as 'Hell made of timber and iron-work thereto, with Divels to the number of 13'. At the parish church of All Hallows, Sherborne, the Easter Sepulchre had a door, the lock and key for which cost 4d in 1514, and it also had a richly carved canopy which cost 6d for cleaning and scouring in 1514. Watch was kept at the sepulchre and at All Hallows the watchmen were allowed 6d as well as ale and fire of coals to keep them warm. Other early liturgical drama was concerned with the Nativity, especially with the coming of the shepherds to the stable, and gradually during the Middle Ages other 'miracle' plays became popular such as the 'Harrowing of Hell' or a Passion Play. These in turn merged into the famous late medieval plays and pageants such as those of Chester, Coventry, Beverley, York and other places.

There were few sermons during the early Middle Ages, though the priest sometimes taught the elements of the faith from the chancel steps, but it is significant that there are no pulpits dating from earlier than the mid-fourteenth century. The sermon was not a regular part of Sunday worship, and many of the clergy were not sufficiently educated to have done more than occasionally expound the basic tenets of the Christian faith. In any case the absence of pews and seats from the naves of parish churches meant that the congregation had to stand, and a long sermon would hardly have been popular. In the later Middle Ages, however, sermons became increasingly common, coinciding with the introduction of seats into the nave, and with the erection of pulpits. The activities and success of the friars with their fiery, lively preaching, racy stories and simple message during the later Middle Ages encouraged many of the parish clergy to emulate them, and led to a marked increase of preaching in parish churches. Devon and Somerset each have more than 35 fine late medieval pulpits, many of them superb works of art in wood or stone, while Gloucestershire has more than 20 late medieval stone pulpits, and there is a notable stone preaching-cross which incorporates a pulpit at Iron Acton (Avon). East Anglia, especially Norfolk, has some superb examples of medieval wooden pulpits, painted with figures of the Evangelists, the saints or with the doctors of the church, but all date from the end of the Middle Ages. For example the hexagonal wooden pulpit at Burnham Norton in Norfolk, with its panels brilliantly painted with the four doctors—St Gregory, St Jerome, St Ambrose and St Augustine— was not installed in the church until the later part of the fifteenth century.

As well as the regular services, the Church was intimately involved in the life of the community through the occasional offices—the services of baptism for the newly-born, marriage, extreme unction for the dying, and burial. Baptism was conducted as soon as possible after birth, often on the same day, and holy water was kept in the locked font so that there should be no delay. For children who might eventually inherit substantial property efforts were made to ensure that the day of baptism should be remembered by local people since in the days before parish registers this was the only way of ensuring that the age of the child could be established. This was very important, since if the child inherited property before attaining the age of twenty-one, he or she became a Ward of the Crown. Occasionally therefore enquiries had to be held to establish proofs of age, and those often give considerable incidental detail about the scene in the parish church on the day of the baptism. For example, John de Welle was born at Bonthorpe in Lincolnshire in 1334 and was baptised in the church of St Helen at Willoughby on the day of his birth. An enquiry 21 years later produced testimony as follows:

John Musters, Knight, aged forty-five years said that he came on the said Tuesday to do fealty to Sir John de Wilughby, Knight, for his lands in Somercotes, and saw the god-mother of the said John, Margaret prioress of Greenfield, carrying him from the said church wrapped in swaddling clothes. Robert de Alford agrees, and says that on the said Tuesday an agreement was made between him and John Jolyf of Willoughby in the said church touching divers trespasses, when the said John son of Adam came there to be baptised.

At Sturminster Marshall (Dorset) the baptism of John Arundell, who was to become lord of the manor, took place in 1408, and when the villagers were questioned about it 21 years later during an enquiry to establish his true age and the legality of his inheritance, they could remember a wealth of detail. It was certainly an eventful day. Walter Russell remembered that he had carried two pots full of wine into the church for the refreshment of the godfathers and the godmother at the baptism. Perhaps others also had some of the wine for John Hekford stated that one Robert Roo had died suddenly in the church, and Richard Pylke remembered that his father was seized with paralysis on that day, and John Garland recalled that he had broken his right arm by falling in the road on his way home from the church. Such a baptism was of course quite exceptional, but since virtually every baby was brought to the parish church to be baptised, the priest came into close personal contact with every family, and the font was an important symbol of the pastoral authority of the parish church. It was for this reason that in countless country churches the ancient font was preserved even when all the rest of the church was rebuilt during the later Middle Ages, so that today the font often provides a clearer indication of the age of the church than almost any other surviving part of its structure. Good examples of this are to be seen in the two Cornish churches of Bodmin and Roche, where the remarkably fine Norman fonts are much earlier than the structure of the present churches within which they are situated. Some evidence of the importance accorded to the sacrament of baptism can also be seen in the prominence given to the font in some churches, especially in East Anglia. Here the fine fonts, often elaborately carved with the seven sacraments and with their towering wooden covers, dominate the western end of the churches. Of many Norfolk examples those at Walpole St Peter and Walsoken may be mentioned, or Salle where the enormous font-cover requires a wooden crane to lift it. Font-covers which could be locked were required during the Middle Ages to ensure that the holy water within was not stolen and put to superstitious uses.

The parish priest was also brought into contact with his people through the marriage service. A marriage was of course a legal contract as well as a sacrament. It consisted of two parts; the first took place at the church door where the actual marriage was performed, and the newly wedded couple then came into church for the nuptial mass. After the mass a loving-cup was passed around among the couple and their guests. These cups were known as 'masers', and an excellent example survives in the church at Buckland in north Gloucestershire. Many others are listed in medieval parish church inventories, for example at Pilton (Somerset) the churchwardens in 1508 possessed 'One stonding maser to serve for Brydes at theyr weddying.' The loving-cup or 'maser' contained wine in which small cakes or wafers called 'sops' were soaked, and as late as 1569 the church wardens of St James, Bristol, paid 2s 6d 'for the little table to dress sops in wyne at any wedding.'

The sacrament of Extreme Unction, which was accompanied by the anointing of the sick person with holy oil, was regarded as of great importance. The Blessed Sacrament was reserved in churches to be immediately available in case of need, and churches also possessed receptacles for the holy oil which was blessed by the diocesan bishop each year on Maunday Thursday and sent out to the parishes in the diocese. Here again the parish priest was an important participant in a crucial event in the life of his parishioners. He was required to go with the sacrament to the dying at any time of the day or night, and at All Hallows', Sherborne, as in many other places, the priest was preceeded through the streets and lanes of the little town by two bedesmen from the almshouse, for whom in 1515 the churchwardens purchased 'a lantern to go with the Sacrament 7d' as well as a handbell to warn passers by of their approach so that they might make due reverence to the priest bearing the Sacred Host. Myrc in his *Instructions for Parish Priests* c.1400, to which reference has already been made, told his readers to be sure that their parishioners knelt as a priest passed by with the Sacred Host on his way to administer Extreme Unction.

> Teche them also I thee pray,
> That when they walken in ye way,
> And see ye preste agayne them comynge,
> Goddes body wythe hym berynge,
> Then wythe grete devocyone,
> Teche them there to kneele downe,
> Fayre ne fowle, spare they nought
> To worship hym that alle hathe wroughte.

Contemporary medieval accounts say comparatively little about burials except that churchwardens' accounts record payments from the relatives of deceased persons for tolling the bells at funerals or for the use of the cross, candlesticks and other articles of the church. The vicar of Yeovil in 1458 paid the churchwardens 3s 4d for letting him borrow the cross, cope and censer from the church when he attended the funeral of the rector of neighbouring Barwick, and several persons paid small sums for knells and for the use of the processional cross and other ornaments of the church at funerals. At St Edmund's, Salisbury, the medieval churchwardens' accounts show constant payments for the 'forthfare' bell which was tolled upon the death of any parishioner, and invited all to pray for the soul of the deceased and to think upon their own end. Knells were also rung upon the bells to commemorate the death of parishioners or of any prominent individual. The churchwardens of St Edmund's also received fees for the hire of the ornaments of the church at funerals—the cross, candlesticks and pall—as well as payments from the relatives of those who were actually buried inside the church. Most burials were, however, in the churchyard, and a few were marked by wooden crosses, but generally graves were not distinguished in this way, and the practice of erecting memorial stones upon graves did not become a common practice until the end of the seventeenth century. In most parishes the same part of the churchyard was used over and over again for burials, any bones which were dug up being deposited in the bone or charnel-house in the churchyard, a good example of which survives in the north-west corner of the churchyard at Mere (Wiltshire) and at Hythe, Kent, while remains of the former charnel house can still be seen at St Peter's Church, St Albans. At Bridgwater, where space in the churchyard was restricted, the churchwardens' accounts record the building of a charnel-house on the north side of the church in 1386. Several churches possessed crypts in which bones were deposited, and examples survive at Elsing (Norfolk) and at Oundle (Northamptonshire), at Westbury-on-Trym and St Mary Redcliffe in Bristol and at Bruton in Somerset, while St Thomas' church in Salisbury possessed a 'Skull house' in which bones were kept. Richer persons paid for the privilege of being buried inside the church. For example at Morebath in north Devon in 1532 the churchwardens' accounts record that 'John Norman at Wode was buryed yn the yle before Sent Sydwyll the viii day of February, for which grave was paid 6s 8d'. Much more common was the payment of a small sum either to have the bells tolled on a particular day a month or a year after the funeral or to have the name of the deceased remembered at the altar, especially upon the anniversary of his or her death. For example at Tintinhull in 1464 Agnes Bretyll left 6s 8d to be prayed for in the church on the anniversary of her death; and at Yeovil in 1519 Margaret Selle of Preston paid 6s 8d for her husband to be remembered at Mass, 'to sett her husband in the comen mynd'. It was this desire to be remembered in the prayers of the church that led to the establishment of so many chantries both in parish churches and in cathedrals during the fifteenth century. A chantry was essentially an endowment, generally of lands, from which the income went to pay a priest to say masses every day for the repose of the soul of the founder and for the souls of all the departed. The great majority of people, who were unable to afford the very heavy expenditure of founding a private chantry, could nonetheless participate in the benefits by joining a gild or association and sharing in the establishment of a communal or gild chantry. Private and gild chantries were commonly established inside parish churches or in chapels or aisles attached to parish churches. In the large church at Bitton in Avon there is a chapel founded in 1299 for the repose of the souls of his parents by Thomas de Bytton, a local boy who rose through the church to become Bishop of Exeter; while at Bromham (Wiltshire) the highly decorated south aisle of the chancel was built as a chantry by William Beauchamp during the fifteenth century. By the end of the Middle Ages there were few churches without their chantry chapel and chantry priest, and many churches contained several chantries. Town churches like those of Ludlow, Coventry, Stamford, Bristol, Norwich and elsewhere were filled with the chantry chapels of the various trade gilds whose enthusiasm for their parish churches and rivalry with each other led to ever more lavish expenditure and sumptuous decoration. The number of altars which formerly existed in parish churches can often still be seen from the 'piscina' or drain at which the priest washed his hands and cleaned the sacred vessels during mass, and which survive in large numbers in many parish churches in side chapels, aisles and occasionally in the nave or even in the tower.

The great number of choir-stalls for the clergy in some churches is also a reminder of the number of chantry priests who were employed. For example St Botolph's at Boston or St Lawrence's at Ludlow both have fine ranges of stalls, and at the latter church no less than seven priests were employed by one of the gilds, that of the Palmers, while at Kings Lynn, by the end of the Middle Ages there were 14 chantry chaplains. In 1410 the parish church of St Bartholomew at Tong in Shropshire was converted into a collegiate church by Dame Isabel Pembridge or Pembrugge, who arranged for a warden and four other priests; at North Cadbury in Somerset a similar collegiate church was established in 1423 by another wealthy and pious lady, Elizabeth de Botreaux. Schools were attached to some chantry foundations, for saying his daily mass would occupy only a little of the time of a chantry priest. The chantry of the Guild of the Holy

Cross in the church of St Martin in Birmingham had a school attached to it which was later to become the school of King Edward VI. In a few cases the fame of the schools has completely overshadowed the chantry foundations of which they were once an adjunct, as has happened with the colleges of St Mary at Winchester and Eton.

Another development of the later Middle Ages was the setting up of private oratories or chapels in private houses, and the creation of chapels-of-ease or subsidiary churches in the outlying parts of large parishes, where the inhabitants found it difficult to get to their parish church. For example in 1308 Sir Simon de Montacute was granted a licence by the Bishop of Exeter 'to build an Oratory in his manor of La More in the parish of Luppitt' and to have divine service celebrated there, although baptisms, marriages and burials had still to be conducted in the parish church. Such private oratories and chapels-of-ease were especially common in some of the large moorland parishes of Devon and Cornwall, and successive Bishops of Exeter granted many such licences: Bishop Brantyngham (1370–94) licensed over 130 such chapels in Devon alone, and Bishop Stafford (1395–1421) granted more than 100 licences. By the end of the Middle Ages the large parish of Hartland in Devon had ten subsidiary chapels in various parts of the parish as well as the stately parish church of St Nectan and the monastery of regular canons; Tiverton had six daughter chapels, and many large parishes had one or more. The large parish of Crewkerne in Somerset was surrounded by a ring of subsidiary churches or chapels—Wayford, Misterton, Seaborough and others, which gradually acquired the dignity of separate parochial status for themselves. At Yetminster in north Dorset the ancient parish which originated as a Saxon 'minster' gradually lost a whole string of subsidiary churches through the Middle Ages and later as its daughter churches—Ryme Instrinseca, Leigh, Chetnole, Lillington and Beer Hackett—became parishes in their own right. Chewton Mendip in Avon was throughout much of the Middle Ages an enormous parish with daughter churches at Farrington Gurney, Paulton, Emborough, Ston Easton and Easton Major. Gradually each of these places became separate parishes, but the parish church at Chewton Mendip is still the focal point for a network of roads, trackways and footpaths which once brought worshippers for special services from the far-flung corners of the original parish. All this was part of the long process of the spread of Christianity and of churches into every corner of the region. The growth in the number of churches in Dorset, for example, can be traced through the Middle Ages, from the 171 listed in 1291, to 218 in 1341 and finally 234 by the time of Henry VIII's enquiry into the wealth of the church, the *Valor Ecclesiasticus* of 1535. Two of the finest churches in England, St Mary Redcliffe in Bristol and Holy Trinity at Hull were both chapels, the one of Bedminster and the other of Hessle. At Newcastle-upon-Tyne the churches of St Andrew, All Saints and St John were all subsidiary chapelries of the parish church of St Nicholas. In the large moorland parishes of west Yorkshire there were also many parochial chapels, and Halifax, for example, was surrounded by subsidiary chapels.

Often the daughter churches continued to pay respect to their original parish church through some annual ceremony or offering. At Crewkerne the parishioners of Seaborough brought the key of their church each year on the day of the patronal festival and solemnly laid it on the high altar. St Stephen in Brannel in mid-Cornwall had two daughter churches, St Dennis and St Michael Caerhayes; even after the Reformation the parishioners of St Dennis continued to pay homage to their mother church and to bring each year on St Stephen's day one pound of beeswax and a black sheep as an offering. The churchwardens of St Thomas-by-Launceston offered annually a wax candle on the high altar of their mother church of St Stephen's-by-Launceston on the day of the patronal festival; and there are many other similar examples. Those who worshipped in the daughter churches of Halifax were obliged to render tithes and oblations to the mother church, and to attend the services at Halifax upon the patronal festival of All Saints.

About the clergy and the other parish officials it is impossible to generalize, since they varied so much in their ability and efficiency. Details of those who behaved badly monopolise the surviving documentary evidence, for the well-behaved are much less likely to appear in official, legal records, so that a superficial examination reveals a great deal wrong with the church, as well as creating a totally false impression, for the evil-doers naturally figure much more prominently than the multitude of quiet conscientious clergy living peaceably in their parishes and ministering to their congregations. The bishops' registers are full of evidence of clerical lapses or irregularities; pluralism, non-residence or the constant reminders of human frailties amongst men who were, for the most part, little different from their parishioners in learning or standards, and who were often ill-paid, were compelled to remain unmarried, and who can only seldom have had much contact either with their fellow clergy or with the bishop and other highly placed officials of the church.

Many of the parish clergy who actually lived and worked in the parishes, as distinct from the non-resident benefice-holders or the clergy attached to cathedrals or to the bishops' households, seem to have been local men, who were probably only slightly better educated than their parishioners and probably differed little from them in outlook. Their interests may have been a little wider and their aspirations a little higher, but most of the clergy were only slightly better off than their parishioners, and they were equally dependent upon the soil for their livelihood and equally at the mercy of agricultural uncertainties. There were many like Richard Fanellor, the rector of Chilton Foliat in Wiltshire, during the late fourteenth century. He was a local man who kept in touch with his family, farmed his own glebe land, and when he died in 1397 directed that he should be buried in his church, that £5 10s 0d should be spent on his funeral, and left gifts and legacies in his will to his three sisters, to his shepherd and to several other servants, as well as to the fabric of the cathedral at Salisbury and to his own church at Chilton Foliat. His executors were his colleague and near neighbour the vicar of Ramsbury and his own stipendiary chaplain or curate. The houses of the clergy also differed little from those of their congregations, and many descriptions of medieval parsonage houses reflect the agricultural preoccupations of the clergy. For example the rectory at Glentham in Lincolnshire in 1305 included an ox-house, cart-house, hay-house and sheepfold all thatched with reed; and a vicarage newly-built at Theddlethorpe in the same county at the end of the fourteenth century had a stable for three horses, a haystore and other farm buildings as well as a sty for 12 pigs.

In their failings also the clergy probably differed very little from their parishioners, with the same boisterous and violent attitudes; like the early fourteenth-century incident at St Buryan when 11 neighbouring incumbents burst open the door of the church and assaulted the Dean of St Buryan and his attendants, beating them so severely that they were in danger of their lives; or the dispute at Sherborne during the 1430s between on the one hand the clergy and townsfolk of the parish church of All Hallows, and on the other the monks of the Benedictine Abbey, a quarrel which led to the deliberate setting fire to the abbey church. In 1306 the Bishop of Exeter had to rebuke the clergy of his diocese for indulging in merry-making and horse-play which went to the extent of mocking the divine service. Such incidents were, naturally, rare; much more common were such clerical lapses as non-residence, failure to conduct all the

4. *The South Doorway, Kilpeck, Herefordshire* The exuberant decoration on this twelfth-century doorway shows a remarkable mixture of Christian and pre-Christian symbolism.

5. (LEFT) *Men Fighting a Two-Headed Monster, Crowcombe, Somerset* Another bench-end of 1534; note that the foliage emerges from the mouth of another monster, while more sinister figures are depicted below. **6.** (RIGHT) *Saxon Doorway, Breamore, Hampshire* The Anglo-Saxon inscription means 'Here the Covenant is shown forth to thee'.

7. *Font from Southrop, Gloucestershire* This elaborately carved Norman font shows the Virtues triumphing over their contrary Vices. Here Patience (Paciencia) is subduing Wrath (Ira), while above are the heavenly mansions. Note that the names of the Vices are carved in mirror-writing as a further indication of their evil.

8. *The Shrine of St Wite or St Candida, Whitechurch Canonicorum, Dorset* A rare survival of a complete stone altar-shrine dating from the thirteenth century, and still containing relics of the saint.

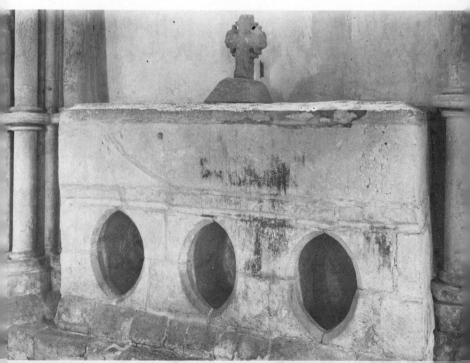

services adequately or to teach the faith properly. In 1301 the vicar of St Mary Church in Devon was reported to the Bishop for being often absent from his parish, for neglecting the fabric and furnishings of the church and for allowing his livestock to pasture in the churchyard, though in his defence it was pointed out that he did preach well and conducted the services admirably when he was there. In 1311 the Bishop of Salisbury reproved several of the Dorset clergy for non-residence, failure to ensure that their churches were in good repair, or for other failings; in particular the rector of Winterborne Stickland, who was a foreigner, was ordered to find a chaplain who could teach him the English language.

But for the most part it seems that the medieval parish clergy performed their duties well. It is impossible to know just what standards of life and work they set themselves, or how they interpreted the requirements of their calling. The fact that so many of the parish clergy perished in the plagues of the fourteenth century is some indication that they were in their parishes and in contact with the sick and dying during the onslaughts of the epidemic. In Wiltshire, for example, during the decade before the Black Death of 1349 the annual number of new institutions of parish clergy was never higher than 40 in a single year; in 1349 it rose to over 100. Ten years later when pestilence again ravaged the land, the annual number of institutions again climbed to more than 100. Similarly in Cornwall the average number of institutions to beneficices per annum in the decade before 1349 was five, and the number had seldom risen above ten per annum in the previous century; in the year 1349–50 the number rose to 85. A similar pattern is revealed in Dorset where half the parishes in the county lost their incumbents during 1349, the year of the plague—impressive evidence of the diligence of the clergy in carrying out the requirements of their office.

Apart from the parish clergy and the churchwardens, one very important official in parish life was the clerk. Originally he would have been in minor orders and his work would have been to assist the priest in saying the services—indeed, the clerk continued to say the responses and give out the hymns in English churches for many years after the Reformation. In 1480 a London mercer, William Hill, left a bequest in his will to maintain a parish clerk in the church of Moulton in Lincolnshire, and the will sets out the duties of the clerk as follows:

. . . to helpe to synge or saye divine service and also to go with the priest when he shall be called to housel folkes [i.e. to administer the Sacrament] in the saide parishe . . . to ringe belles and take charge of suche goodes as

belongen to the saide cherche and keepe the keys of the same by the discre-
tion of thrifty men of the same parishe.

At Yetminster in Dorset the clerk had the task of ringing one of the church
bells at dawn and dusk each day, being paid for this task by the income
from lands in the parish which continued until recent times to bear the
name 'Curfew lands'. A dispute over the duties and remuneration of the
clerk at Morebath in north Devon in 1536 has left a record of the work
done by the clerk there. He was expected to be present at the services, to
attend to the vestments and to dress the altars. He was to help the incumbent at Mass and with the occasional offices. The clerk was also expected
to take charge of the church key and to open and shut the church at
reasonable times. Once a year he was to go around the parish with holy
water to bless the crops; and after sheep-shearing he was to go around the
parish to collect stray bits of wool to make a coat for himself in the parish's
own livery. Besides his livery, the parish clerk at Morebath was entitled
to 'a stitch of clean corn of every householder'—that is ten sheaves—and
occasionally also the parish held a special church ale, known as a 'clerk's
ale', the proceeds of which went to the parish clerk.

2. Building, decoration and furnishing

There is little surviving documentary evidence of the way in which the earliest parish churches were built, or of how the necessary money was raised. Not until copious written records become available during the fifteenth century in the form of churchwardens' accounts, contracts and other documentary evidence, is it possible to be certain just how the whole complicated business of fund-raising and construction was organised. During the early centuries of Christianity the principal part in church-building was taken by the lords of manors who built churches for their tenants, or by zealous missionary priests who organised and superintended the work. For example St Aldhelm, the first bishop of Sherborne, who died in 709, is said to have built churches at Bradford-on-Avon, Bruton and Wareham; in the early tenth century St Dunstan caused the church at Glastonbury to be greatly extended, and many of the local saints of Devon and Cornwall are credited with the erection of churches. William of Malmesbury records how a church at York which had previously been built by King Edwin who had been inspired by St Paulinus, had fallen into ruin and was rebuilt and restored by St Wilfrid in c 690; and how St Wilfrid also built churches at Ripon and Hexham. An inscription on a sundial now above the south porch of the church at Kirkdale in the North Riding of Yorkshire records that 'Orm son of Gamal bought St Gregory's minster when it was all ruined and fallen down and caused it to be built afresh from the foundation (in honour of) Christ and St Gregory in the days of King Edward and in the days of Earl Tosti.' At Weaverthorpe, Yorkshire, an inscription on the church records that it was built during the early years of the twelfth century at the cost of Herbert the Chamberlain, an official in the court of Henry I. The involvement of local lords meant that they and their successors retained the 'advowson' or right to appoint the rector to their churches, and explains why so much church patronage remained in the hands of the nobility and gentry. It may also explain why

35

so frequently in many parts of the country the parish church is to be found adjacent to the manor house and at some distance from the village, for the lord built the church on a site conveniently close to his own house.

There is no surviving evidence from the early Middle Ages of participation by ordinary parishioners in church-building, though they may well have contributed money, labour or materials for which no records survive. Once the church was built and a parish was recognised with its own priest, then the laity were of necessity involved both in attending the services and in contributing tithes and other offerings for the maintenance of the priest. Neither is there any surviving early evidence for parish churches of how suitably skilled workmen were obtained or of how the building work was planned and organised, although such evidence does exist for some of the cathedrals and abbeys.

In contrast to this paucity of material for the early Middle Ages, there is no lack of detailed evidence for the fifteenth century. From church-wardens' accounts, building contracts, descriptions and other records we can be quite clear about the way in which the great surge of church-building in the century and a half before the Reformation was organised and financed. As in previous centuries, some churches were rebuilt, enlarged or adorned wholly or largely at the expense of one individual or one family. For example, Elsing church, Norfolk, was built during the fourteenth century by Sir Henry Hastings who was later buried in the chancel, and Northleach church in Gloucestershire was reconstructed at the cost of the wool merchant John Fortey who died in 1458, and besides his brass memorial the church also contains several other memorials to men who had grown rich in the wool trade and who had lavished money on the church. Fairford church in Gloucestershire was rebuilt in the latest style during the 1490s by the Tame family, who were wealthy wool merchants there; the costs of rebuilding the superb church at Steeple Ashton in Wiltshire were largely borne by the Long family who were also engaged in the wool and cloth trade. At Piddletrenthide in Dorset a new aisle was added to the church during the fifteenth century by the Collier family who leased the demesne lands there from Winchester College. The church at North Cadbury in Somerset with its large chancel was rebuilt by Lady Elizabeth Botreaux early in the fifteenth century and was intended to serve as a college of secular priests or canons. Richard Carew wrote of how the Cornish church of Sheviocke was rebuilt by the Dawnay family who were lords of the manor there, who at the same time had a barn built nearby, and that 'casting up their accounts upon finishing of their works, the barn was found to cost three halfpence more than the church; and so it might well fall out, for it is a great barn and a little church'.

Many other churches throughout the country were built or greatly enlarged at the expense of one or two individuals or families, like the clothiers Thomas Spring and Simon Branch who together with the Earl of Oxford built the magnificent church at Lavenham in Suffolk, or the merchants who were responsible for the fine churches at Patrington, Hull and Boston. Anthony Ellis, a successful wool merchant of Great Ponton in Lincolnshire, built the tower of the church there with the inscription 'Thinke and Thanke God for all'. The massive late medieval tombs of such families as the Cobhams at Cobham in Kent or the Harcourts at Stanton Harcourt in Oxfordshire, show clearly who was responsible for those churches.

Nonetheless, in spite of the many examples of family or individual generosity in church-building, most parishes did not have the advantage of wealthy benefactors, and in the majority of places the enlargement, rebuilding, decoration and furnishing of the parish churches took place at the expense of the parishioners themselves, and was paid for with money slowly collected by the sort of parish activities which will be described in the next chapter.

The main feature that emerges from any examination of the late medieval evidence is how frequently the rebuilding or enlargement of the parish church was entirely due to the enthusiasm and generosity of the whole community in the parish. Whatever their motives—and these no doubt ranged from simple enthusiasm for the project, through local rivalry with neighbouring parishes over the size and splendour of the parish churches or the height and magnificence of their towers, to sheer concern for personal salvation and an understandable desire to avoid the torments of the sort of hell so frequently and vividly depicted in late medieval imagery—there is no doubt that incredibly large sums of money were raised from innumerable poor and thinly populated parishes. Perhaps the best surviving documentary evidence of this comes from Bodmin in Cornwall. During the second half of the fifteenth century much of the church in the little town was rebuilt, the old Norman structure was ruthlessly demolished and replaced by a grand new church in the latest style; similar rebuildings and enlargements occurred throughout the country, but what makes the events at Bodmin so important is the fact that the complete building-account survives, covering the years 1469 to 1472. This remarkable piece of evidence shows how the whole project was organised by the church wardens. Money was raised by the sale of parts of the old church; for example windows, presumably stained-glass windows, were sold to nearby parishes, St Kew and Helland; gifts of both money and goods were received; house-to-house collections were organised; and, above all, money came in from parish functions and especially from fund-raising carried out by the numerous local gilds during their annual Whitsuntide celebrations. The money was carefully stored by the churchwardens until there was sufficient for rebuilding to commence. Stone was obtained from the nearby moorland, and higher quality granite from Pentewan on the coast near St Austell. The way in which the stone was brought to Bodmin from the quarries at Pentewan illustrates some of the difficulties which medieval builders faced in the transport of their materials, for in order to avoid the difficult overland journey across the high moorland of mid-Cornwall the Bodmin churchwardens arranged for the stone to be transported by barge across St Austell bay to Fowey and thence up the river Fowey to Lostwithiel; there it was loaded on to waggons and wains for the final part of the journey to Bodmin. Timber, both for the church itself and for all the necessary scaffolding, was obtained locally, some of it being given by local landowners. Much of the building work was also done by local workmen, but for the roof and the doorways and windows masons and carpenters were obtained from as far away as Exeter, and accommodation had to be provided for them in Bodmin while they worked on the new church. Large numbers of workmen were employed on the project, for there was little mechanical assistance apart from a crane and bucket.

From the detailed Bodmin accounts we can calculate that the total cost of the work amounted to £268 17s 9½d, excluding all the materials and labour contributed by local people for which no charge was made. It cannot be too often emphasised that, whatever the motives of the donors, the raising of such large sums for parish churches in so many parishes was an immense achievement, and is impressive evidence of the communal desire to make their churches as large and opulent as possible, and of the strength of religious faith which could lead such relatively poor communities to devote so much of their material wealth to the greater glory of God. In the same way the superb spire at Louth (Lincolnshire) was built between 1501 and 1515 entirely by the enthusiasm and money-raising zeal of the parishioners, the total cost of £305 7s 5d being raised by gifts and collections and, above all, by contributions by the gilds of the little town. Their generosity created one of the most graceful of English spires reaching to a height of 295 ft. The Louth accounts reveal something of the passionate concern of churchwardens and parishioners for the adornment of their churches, for they did not scruple to get themselves heavily into debt, borrowing money from various sources so that the work of building could continue. As in so many other places, the ultimate responsibility both for money-raising and for the supervision of the project rested upon the churchwardens, who were obviously totally committed and dedicated to the work. Their accounts show the difficulties which they had with their master mason. In 1505 Christopher Scune was appointed master mason, but as he was also in charge of major works at Ripon and Durham, he came to Louth very seldom. The resident mason at Louth, in charge of day-to-day affairs, was a local man Laurence Lemying. As the work proceeded the churchwardens found it increasingly difficult to get Scune to come to Louth, and finally after increasingly urgent appeals had been sent to him he was sacked and replaced by a master mason from Boston, John Tempas. Finally in 1515 the spire was finished and the church-wardens triumphantly recorded in their accounts:

The 15th Sunday after Holy Trinity of the year (1515) the weathercock was set upon the broach of Holy Rood Eve after, there being William Ayleby parish priest, with many of his brethren priests there present, hallowing the said weathercock and the stone that it stands upon, and so conveyed upon the said broach; and the said priests singing Te Deum Laudamus, with organs, and then the kirkwardens garred ring all the bells, and caused all the people there being to have bread and ale; and all to the loving of God, our Lady and All Saints.

The enthusiasm of the town gilds at Ludlow during the fifteenth century contributed largely to the rebuilding and enlargement of the parish church, and the same was true of countless other English towns and villages.

The money for building the tower of the church at Eye in Suffolk in 1470 was 'gatheryd that yere partly with the plough, partly in church ales, partly in legacies given that way but chiefly of the frank and devoute hartes of the people', and amounted to 'the sum of £40 and litell odde money'.

Among the records of Totnes in Devon the account survives of how the tower of the parish church was built there during the 1440s. The old bell-tower had been made of wood, and this was demolished and the wood sold. Collections and fund-raising activities were organised, particularly collections in the church on Sundays, known as 'Sunday pence' and, in addition, the parishioners themselves worked in a nearby quarry digging stone for the new tower. This gesture was not entirely voluntary, for in 1448 it was recorded that those who refused to take part in the work or who refused to contribute to the regular Sunday collections were to have their names reported to the Archdeacon's court. Again, the difficulties of transport are apparent; the quarry was near the river and the stone was brought to Totnes by barge, and thence had to be carried by the parishioners to the churchyard.

The way in which local rivalry between parishes contributed to the late medieval burst of church-building and tower-construction is perhaps evident in the fact that before work started the churchwardens travelled around a large surrounding area to Tavistock, Callington and elsewhere, to 'view divers bell towers in the country' to get ideas as to the sort of tower they would like. Roger Growdone, master mason, was then appointed to supervise the work of the building. Here again, however, as at Bodmin and scores of other places, it is clear that the whole project was a community effort, and that whatever motives or pressures were involved, it was paid for by the parishioners themselves.

A contract for building a tower at Walberswick church in Suffolk in 1425 specifies that the general design was to be like that of Tunstall while the windows were to be like those in the tower at Halesworth. In the same way a contract for building a tower at Helmingham in Suffolk made in 1487 specified that it should have the best features of two neighbouring towers, 'a sufficient newe stepyll of LX fote of heythe after the brede wydness and thicknesse of the stepyll of Framesden . . . . so that it be mayd after the facion of the stepyll of Bramston. . . .' An agreement with a mason to make battlements all the way around the church at Orby in Lincolnshire in 1529 specified that the battlements around the church itself should be similar to those at Weston Admeals and those around the tower like the ones at East Keal.

When the parishioners of Dunster in west Somerset decided to add a tower to their parish church in 1442, the project was a communal enterprise arranged by the churchwardens on behalf of the entire parish. The contract survives for the Dunster tower, and this shows that while the actual building was to be carried out by a local mason, John Marys of Stogursey, the materials, stone and wood, were to be provided by the parish and brought to the churchyard. Other points of interest emerge from the Dunster contract. John Marys was evidently allowed considerable latitude in the manner of construction so long as it was done 'after reason and good proportion'; apparently only the design of the tower-windows was precisely stipulated and these were to be according to the pattern or design made by one Richard Pope, freemason or architect. It is also clear from the contract that few men were to be involved in the building-work on the tower, and that there was little mechanical assistance, for the stipulation was made that if any of the stones were so large that John Marys and his two or three workmen could not lift it, then the parish was to provide additional muscle power; 'Allso if there be any stone y wroughte of such quantity that ii men or iii at moste may not kary (carry) hym the sayde parishe shall helpe hym'. According to the terms of the contract John Marys was to be paid for his work on the tower at the rate of 13s 4d per foot, excluding the materials.

Many of the finest west-country towers were still being built when the Reformation occurred. For example, at Chewton Mendip in Somerset money was still being given to complete the superb tower there during the 1540s, and several other of the magnificent towers of Somerset were still unfinished at that time. In 1602 Richard Carew commented on the finest of all the Cornish towers, Probus, and wrote that the 'high and fair church tower of hewed moorstone was builded within compass of our rememberance by the well disposed inhabitants'.

At the same time that parishes were lavishing money on the structure of their churches, they were also engaged in other expensive communal work such as the building of church-houses and the decoration and furnishing of the interior of the churches. At Bodmin, for example, as soon as building-work on the church was completed, the churchwardens embarked upon further fund-raising in order to equip the church with appropriate vestments, plate, wall-paintings and glass, as well as with an elaborately carved and costly rood-screen, and with pews throughout the nave. Evidence for the way in which additions to the interior furnishing of parish churches were made survives in the churchwardens' accounts of Yatton in Avon. The accounts reveal a remarkably active church life, with tremendous fund-raising activity by this little community. The money was spent on the enlargement and maintenance of the large and ornate parish church. In 1446 the Yatton churchwardens started upon a new project, one which was carried out in almost all west-country parish churches during the fifteenth century, the construction of an elaborate rood-screen dividing off the chancel from the nave, and surmounted by the rood—the figure of the crucified Christ with the attendant figures of the Blessed Virgin and St John. At Yatton the large screen went across both the nave and the two aisles, and had a large loft above the screen on which an organ was later mounted. The first task of the churchwardens, once it had been decided to build a rood screen, was to examine other screens in the locality to get ideas as to the form and shape which would best suit their church. Their accounts record expenses incurred in travelling to local churches including those in Bristol and Easton-in-Gordano, to view the screens. Next, timber had to be purchased, and oak was obtained from as far away as the forest of Selwood on the borders of Somerset and Wiltshire. The work itself was entrusted to a local craftsman, John Crosse who, with his apprentice ('hys childe') worked for several years on the construction and carving of the elaborate screen. From time to time Crosse was encouraged in his work, not just by money payments, but as in 1454 by 'ale gevyn to Crosse at certyn tymis yn hys worke to make hym well wellede'. When the screen was finished and erected in the church it had then to be painted, and the accounts record large expenditure on paint in Bristol and payments to the painter for his work and for his accommodation. Finally, 69 statues of the Saints were bought to stand on the rood-screen. Here again we have an example of a genuine communal effort all directed towards the beautifying of the parish church.

At Tintinhull in Somerset the churchwardens raised money by church ales, gifts, collections and by hiring out the church-house for wedding feasts and other functions. During the 1450s they had built and decorated a rood-screen and loft, of wihch the lower stage, built of local stone, survives. Later they spent money on having the height of the tower increased, on a stair-turret for the tower, on a porch, and on having seats put into the nave.

At St Mary-at-Hill in London in 1426 the sum of £29 4s 2d was collected to build a roof and screen and loft in the church; 70 years later in 1496 the loft was reconstructed at a cost of £7. Several 'Karvers' were employed 'for makyng of the fygyrres' and the entries in the churchwardens accounts for 1496 also include:

To the Karvare for makyng of iii dyadems and one of the Evangelystes, and for mendyng the Roode, the Crosse, the Mary and John, the Crown of Thorn with ad other fawles. 10s
To Undirwood for payntyng and gyldynge of the Roode, the Crosse, Mary and John, the iiii Evangelystes and iii dyadems   .   .   . £5.0.0.

All the surviving pre-Reformation churchwardens' accounts contain similar examples, and there is no reason to suppose that these parishes were in any way different from the host of others for which documentary evidence does not exist.

The way in which well-designed screens as well as towers, windows and other features of churches might be copied by neighbouring parishes for many miles around has already been noted. This process is well illustrated in the contract for constructing a rood-screen and loft at Stratton (Cornwall) in 1531. The contract was made between the church-wardens of Stratton and two carpenters, John Dawe of Lawhitton (Corn-wall) and John Pares of North Lew (Devon); it was stipulated that the rood-loft was to be made like that of St Kew, the rood itself with the attendant figures of the Blessed Virgin and St John was to be like that in Liskeard church, the two altars before the rood-screen were to be like those of St Kew, and other features of the screen and of the new windows which were to be made to throw light on it were to copy those at Week St Mary church. The rood-lofts were used for various purposes. That regular access to them was required is evident from the fact that many churches have specially constructed stone stairways leading to the rood-loft; and in many cases the stairways survive even where the rood-screens and lofts have long since been demolished. Larger churches often had an organ, always described as 'a pair of organs', on the rood-loft. The church-wardens of St Margarets, Westminster, in 1478–80 paid for 'a dore in the Rode lofte to save and keep people from the organys'. At Wimborne Minster in Dorset 11d was paid in 1495 for 'glyw and lether' for the organs in the rood-loft; and late medieval inventories commonly refer to the organs in the rood-loft. Occasionally also a choir or singers were accom-modated in the loft, or the gospel was read from it. At St Mary-at-Hill in 1501 12d was paid for 'makyng of a lectorne in the Rood loft', and at Ranworth in Norfolk the fifteenth-century lectern, which was formerly in the rood-loft, is still to be found in the church, and has painted upon it the musical notation for part of the mass. In most small parish churches, however, neither the rood-loft nor the church itself was suitable for singing or reading from such a position, but access to the rood was still required in order to attend to the candles burning before the figures, and for covering the figures with a veil during Lent. At Pilton in Somerset in 1508 the churchwardens bought 'xii ellys of lenyn clothe for the Rode lofte vii s vii d.' together with rings, staples and cords for the Lent cloth. Occasionally the iron-work or pulleys for the Lent-cloth or for the lights hanging before the rood survive, as at St Peter Mancroft, Norwich, and Orchardleigh in Somerset. Nowhere, however, do the figures that formerly stood upon the rood-screen remain in their original position.

Like the churches themselves, the interior furnishings and decoration came partly from the gifts of individuals and of specific groups like gilds, or they were the result of a communal effort by the whole parish. The magnificent glass at Fairford in Gloucestershire came from the generosity of the Tame family; John Cantelow, the prior of Bath, gave an east window to the nearby church of St Catherine's; Peter Carslegh, the vicar of Winscombe in Somerset, gave a window to the church there, depicting three different saints who bore his name, Peter. The church at St Neot in Cornwall has some of the finest stained glass in the west country, 15 large windows, filled with colour, depicting scenes from the Old and New Testament, as well as legends of the Cornish saints; these were made at the end of the fifteenth century and owe their existence to various groups in the parish, the wives, young men, young women, etc., who raised the money to pay for them. An inscription on the font at St Mary's, Beverley, shows that it was given by William Fairfax, draper, and his wife in 1530.

In the same way groups of people combined to pay for statues. At Croscombe in Somerset during the fifteenth century there were, as at St Neot, several religious gilds, and one of the gild projects was the purchase of a fine statue of St George for one of the side chapels. It was ordered from a stone carver in Exeter, and more than £27 was spent on the image and its decoration. Most churches had several such statues of the most popular late medieval saints, the Virgin, St John, St Peter, St George, St Christopher and many others, which were the object of particular veneration and devotion. The gilds with their own chapels, and their own feasts and rituals, played a vital part as the focus of religious as well as social life in most parishes, and also contributed immeasurably to the adornment of their churches.

Another project that engaged the energy of many congregations during the years before the Reformation was the provision of pews in the nave of their parish church. Until late in the Middle Ages it was the custom for worshippers either to stand or kneel in church, and in most places fixed seats were not introduced before the second half of the fifteenth century. A few churches had stone benches along the walls or around pillars where the elderly or infirm might rest, and examples can still be seen at Priddy, North Petherton and North Curry in Somerset, Bratton near Westbury and Bishopstone near Salisbury in Wiltshire, Sutton Bonnington, Nottinghamshire, Skirbeck in Lincolnshire, Patrington in Yorkshire and many others. One of the earliest sets of wooden pews are those at Clapton-in-Gordano (Avon) which consist of roughly shaped benches with solid uncarved ends; these probably date from the fourteenth century and are unusually early for a parish church.

Many late medieval pews survive and are of great interest as superb examples of the woodcarver's art, for the practice became common of carving the bench-ends with all sorts of subjects and figures. Many are religious, such as the instruments of the Passion, of which many examples survive, especially in Cornish churches; others show figures of the saints, religious emblems such as the sacred monogram, the pelican, the dove, angels, etc. A large number of bench-ends, however, are carved with completely secular or even pagan subjects: for example, figures of the Green Man or Jack-in-the-Green at Bishops Lydeard, Crowcombe and Monksilver (Somerset); mermaids at Down St Mary (Devon) and Zennor (Cornwall); dancers and jesters from Altarnun and St Levan (Cornwall), Landcross (Devon) and North Cadbury (Somerset); bagpipers from Abbotsham (Devon) and Davidstow (Cornwall), and the series of three bench-ends at South Brent (Somerset) which depict part of the legend of Reynard the Fox. At Blythborough church in Suffolk the bench-ends of c 1475 are carved with representations of the vices—Pride, Gluttony Sloth etc—and with the labours of the months. Occasionally the benches can be precisely dated. Those at Crowcombe and North Cadbury, for example, both bear the date 1534. The pews at Affpuddle in Dorset were provided by a vicar of the parish, who had previously been a monk at the Benedictine monastery of Cerne Abbas before its dissolution in 1539, and one of the pews which he installed at Affpuddle has the inscription 'Thes seatys were mayd in the yere of Oure Lord God MCCCCXLVII the tyme of Thomas Lyllyngton, vicar of this cherche'. Churchwardens' accounts commonly show expenditure upon the provision of seats. For example, at Tintinhull (Somerset) in 1511–12 the churchwardens paid £1 13s 4d to a carpenter for 'sawyng of tymber for seetys (seats) for ye churche and for cuttyng and framyng partt of the same'. These seats survive in the church and have the unusual feature of a flap attached to the end of each pew which can be pulled out to provide an additional seat. At Bodmin in 1491, when it was decided to have pews throughout the nave and a pulpit, the churchwardens contracted with a carpenter Matthy More for the pews and the pulpit at a cost of £92. This contract again reveals the strength of local rivalry and the way in which particularly good designs were copied by other parishes, for the Bodmin churchwardens stipulated that the pews should be like those in the church of St Mary at Plympton (Devon) and that the pulpit should be 'after the furme and making of the pulpyte yn the parysh churche of Mourton yn hemstede [Moretonhampstead, Devon]'.

No sooner had seats appeared in the naves of parish churches than churchwardens saw in them an opportunity of raising funds, and the custom of charging rents for the right to sit in particular pews was started. The churchwardens' accounts of Ludlow and of St Lawrence's, Reading, both show a regular income from pew rents from the mid-fifteenth century. At Yeovil there was a large regular income from pew rents during the late Middle Ages; there was a fixed tariff, so that seats in the front and near the pulpit cost 18d per annum while those at the back cost 6d or less. It is also clear that the men and women sat in separate parts of the church.

From the evidence that survives in the parish churches themselves, as well as from documentary sources, it is possible to make the difficult imaginative leap which is necessary if we are to recreate a picture of the decoration and furnishing of a typical late medieval parish church. Perhaps the most difficult aspect to imagine is the colour, since many parish churches must have been a riot of different colours, with painted stone and woodwork, wall-paintings and stained glass. Enough survives in a few churches, as for example at Copford in Essex, Pickering in Yorkshire, on the painted screens of East Anglia, at Kempley in Gloucestershire, Torbryan in Devon, St Neot in Cornwall, Tarrant Crawford in Dorset or Sutton Bingham in Somerset to show, albeit in a faded and partial way, what many church interiors must have been like; and late medieval churchwardens' accounts show constant payments to painters for decorating all parts of the church. The profusion of lights, altars, screens and statues is also clear from surviving examples and from a few written sources. Occasionally inventories of church goods survive for the later Middle Ages and give an excellent indication of just how much was lost in the destruction and confiscations of the sixteenth century. For example, an inventory dated 1508 exists of the goods in All Hallows church at Sherborne in Dorset, a church formerly attached to the great abbey church there, and which was demolished after the Reformation when the parish obtained the former abbey church. All Hallows possessed numerous crosses, candlesticks, pyxes for the blessed sacrament, a silver pax for the kiss of peace ceremony during Mass, statues, precious stones, rosaries, beads, and other valuable items which had been acquired as gifts over the years, as well as numerous sets of vestments and needlework for the altars etc. At Pilton in Somerset an inventory made in 1509 lists a similar variety of valuable objects, including 15 suits of vestments and more than a dozen mass-books, processionaries, books of chants etc., some printed and some manuscript. A much earlier inventory survives from Kensworth church (which was then in Hertfordshire and is now in Buckinghamshire). This is dated 1297, and shows that the church possessed four surplices, and various other vestments for Sundays and festivals, some of them embroidered; two chalices, one of them of silver; three pyxes or receptacles for the Blessed Sacrament, two of wood and one of ivory; a bell; two statutes of the Blessed Virgin for carrying in procession; and several service books including two missals, a manual, and various other books of psalms, chants and services for particular occasions. Again, there is no suggestion that Kensworth was in any way unusual in its wealth or possessions.

As with so many features of parish churches and parish life, it is impossible to generalise, and there is no doubt that at times during the Middle Ages many churches were very poorly equipped and that some were dilapidated, but there is no reason to suppose that the possessions of churches like All Hallows, Sherborne, Pilton or Kensworth were in any way unusual or extraordinary. What is beyond doubt is the attachment of local people to their parish churches, and their readiness to contribute regular and staggeringly large sums towards their maintenance and decoration and for the purchase of expensive items of equipment. Perhaps nowhere is this better shown than at Morebath, a comparatively poor country parish in north Devon. The churchwardens' accounts for the 1520s, the very eve of the Reformation, include references to gifts of all kinds for the church—livestock such as sheep, bees and pigs, altar cloths, Lent cloths, wedding-rings, coats, dresses and gowns, candlesticks, handkerchiefs and many other articles. The vicar, Christopher Trychay, gave an image of St Sidwell, and one of the parishioners gave her wedding-ring to buy a pair of shoes for the statue; another parishioner made a bequest to keep a light burning before the statue at every principal feast day in the year. Perhaps most remarkable of all was the fact that when, in 1534, the silver chalice of the church was stolen by a thief who climbed on to the roof and in through one of the tower windows, 'ye young men and maydens of ye parysse dru them selffe togethers and with there gyfts and provysyon they bofth (bought) yn another challis without any chargis of ye parysse'. In the same year, 1534, while the parliament at Westminster was passing the Act of Supremacy which effectively abolished the Pope's power in England and brought to an end the thousand year-old link with the Catholic church, the parishioners at Morebath were engaged in reseating their church, all the timber for the work being given by members of the little congregation.

A remarkable description exists of the appearance of Long Melford church in Suffolk just before the Reformation. It was made by Roger Martyn of Melford Place in c 1580 and describes the church as it was in his youth before all the changes of the Reformation period. He remembers first the spectacular glory of the chancel with its painted statues and the elaborate reredos to the high altar and the gilt tabernacle reaching up to the roof. The side altars were also lavishly decorated and furnished with statues. A fine rood screen ran across the whole building surmounted by the figure of the crucified Christ,

. . . a fair Rood Loft, with the Rood, Mary and John, of every side, and with a fair pair of Organs standing thereby . . . the side thereof, towards the body of the church, in twelve partitions in boards, was fair painted with the images of the twelve apostles'. He remembers also the roof of the church 'beautified with fair guilt stars'. The church also possessed 'many rich Copes and Suites of vestments . . . .'

Other things which had evidently impressed him as a boy included the Easter Sepulchre, an elaborate wooden structure which was set up in the chancel on Maundy Thursday; the processions on Palm Sunday, Corpus Christi and Rogation week, and the bonfires and celebrations held to mark St James Eve, Midsummer Eve, the Eve of the feast of St Peter and St Paul, and finally St Thomas Eve when there was bread and ale and 'some long pyes of mutton and peasecods'.

Much of this regular round of ceremonial and festivals together with most of the decoration and valuable possessions of parish churches disappeared or were confiscated by the Crown during the upheavals of the Reformation, and the dramatic effects of this revolution, both upon the appearance of parish churches and upon the life of the parish, will be described in chapter 4.

9. *The Rood Screen, Kenton, Devon* An indication of the exuberance and splendour of west-country wood-carving during the later Middle Ages.

10. *The Rood Screen, Ranworth, Norfolk* Note the profusion of painted figures, the side-screens enclosing two nave altars, and the rare pre-Reformation lectern on the left of the central doorway in the screen.

11. *Ranworth, Norfolk* The painted figure of the Virgin and Child from the Rood screen, an indication of the richness of its decoration and figure-painting.

3. Church and community in the Middle Ages

So far we have looked at the way in which the parish churches served the community through services and prayers; this chapter will be concerned with the parish church as the centre of community life, secular as well as religious, and with the way in which communal events were used to raise money for the repair, extension and adornment of the churches. Again, we are heavily dependent upon documentary sources from the end of the Middle Ages, since there is scarcely any written evidence which relates to parish community life in the early medieval period, or to the way in which the church buildings and their surroundings were used by the parishioners either for devotion or for recreation. A vital role in community life during the later Middle Ages was played by the churchwardens, the chosen representatives of the parish. The Tudor monarchs were to load on to the shoulders of the churchwardens during the sixteenth century a mass of secular duties, but during the Middle Ages their only concern, as their title suggests, was with the parish church, with the maintenance, enlargement and beautifying of the fabric and with the provision of the materials for the services. But the office of churchwarden does not appear until the thirteenth century, and churchwardens' accounts do not survive from earlier than the fourteenth century. How parochial affairs were managed before this time is not clear, although the convention grew up very early that the laity were responsible for the upkeep of the nave of the parish church while the person or institution which held the advowson or patronage of the living was charged with the maintenance of the chancel. It seems probable that in the early Middle Ages a much greater share of the responsibility for day-to-day parochial as well as church affairs fell to the lot of the parish priest. It is also likely that parishioners made use of their parish churches for secular as well as religious meetings, though here also there is little firm evidence from the early medieval period.

By the time that documentary sources become copious, that is from the later fourteenth century, there is abundant evidence of the central part played by the parish churches in the social and communal life of the parish. The main social activity as well as a principal fund-raising operation was the church-ale. This forerunner of the modern garden fete consisted of a parish gathering at which food as well as drink in the form of ale was supplied by the churchwardens, and was accompanied by sports, dancing and other festivities. Originally these gatherings may well have been held in the nave of the church itself, but there is little documentary evidence of this, for by the time that churchwardens' accounts become available the church ales were held either in the open air, or in the church-house which was specially built for parish meetings. One reference which does survive to church ales apparently being held in the church itself is from the churchwardens' accounts of St Lawrence, Reading, and is as late as 1506. The entry reads:

To Macrell for makyng clene of the Church agaynst the day of drinking in the seid Church	4d
For flesh spyce and bakyng of pasteys agaynst the said drynkyng	2s 9½d
For ale at the same drynkyng	1s 5d
For mete and drynke to the Taberer	9d

Since in most country parishes the church ales were the main source of revenue for the churches, references to them are abundant in the surviving churchwardens' accounts, and since church ales continued in the traditional manner for a century or more after the Reformation there are also several descriptions of them and of the way in which they were conducted. Richard Carew in his *Survey of Cornwall* published in 1602 describes the Cornish custom whereby

For the church-ale, two young men of the parish are yerely chosen by their last forerunners to be wardens, who, dividing the task make collection among the parishioners, of whatsoever provision it pleaseth them voluntarily to bestow. This they employ in brewing, baking, and other acates [i.e. provisions bought or provided], against Whitsuntide, upon which holidays the neighbours met at the church house, and there merily feed on their own victuals, each contributing some petty portion to the stock, which, by many smalls, groweth to a meetly greatness; for there is entertayned a kind of emulation between these wardens, who, by his graciousness in gathering, and good husbandry in expending, can best advance the church's profit. Besides, the neighbour parishes at those times lovingly visit one another, and frankly spend their money together. The afternoons are concerned in such exercises as olde and yonge folke (having leysure) doe accustomarly weare out the time withall. When the feast is ended, the wardens yeeld in their accounts to the parishioners; and such money as exceedeth the disbursement is layd up in store, to defray any extraordinary charges arising in the parish, or imposed on them for the good of the countrey or the prince's service; . . .

Later in the seventeenth century John Aubrey, the Wiltshire antiquarian, wrote that

There were no rates for the poor in my grandfather's days; but for Kington St Michael (no small parish) the church ale of Whitsontide did the business. In every parish is (or was) a church-house to which belonged spits, crocks, etc., utensils for dressing provisions. Here the housekeepers met, and were merry, and gave their charity. The young people were there too, and had dancing, bowling, shooting at butts, etc., the ancients sitting gravely by, and looking on. All things were civil, and without scandal.

Any examination of late medieval churchwardens' accounts leaves no doubt of the importance of church ales in raising funds for the church: not only parishioners attended, for often people came from neighbouring parishes to take part in the festivities and also so that their own church ales might in turn be patronised by their neighbours. Some churchwardens obviously felt it their duty to attend neighbouring ales, and charged the expenses in their accounts. For example the churchwardens of Tintinhull in south Somerset attended the church ale of the neighbouring parish of Montacute in 1513 and charged the 1s 8d which they spent there to church expenses; while in 1516 they attended church ales at three nearby parishes, Stoke-sub-Hamdon, Montacute and Chilthorne Domer and charged 6d for their expenses. The churchwardens at Yatton in Avon in 1454 attended the church ale at Wrington and included in their accounts the entry 'for expenses atte Cherche ale of Wryngton 10d.'

There are also many examples of parishes going to considerable trouble to make their ales as grand and attractive as possible, even hiring the regalia and choirs from other parishes to swell their own processions which were often a popular and important part of the proceedings. For example the processional cross, banners, vestments and other regalia from the affluent church at Yeovil were hired for 1s 6d by the parish of Sturminster Newton some 15 miles distant, in 1457, for use at their patronal festival and church ale so as to increase the splendour and attractiveness of the occasion; and the Yeovil regalia was regularly hired by neighbouring parishes. The profits of church ales were frequently very large. At Yatton in Avon the fifteenth-century churchwardens' accounts show a regular annual profit of more than £4.00 from church ales, as well as similar

annual sums received from hiring out the church-house and its utensils
for private functions, especially for wedding feasts. The medieval wooden
gallery at the west end of Cawston church in Norfolk has carved along it
the words 'God spede the plow and send us ale corn enow our purpose to
make at crow of cok of the plowlete of Sygate be merry and glede war
good ale yis work mad'. Whatever the precise meaning of this somewhat
enigmatic inscription, its general message is clear enough that 'good ale
this work made', or that it was erected from the proceeds of church ales.

SECULAR ACTIVITIES

There is probably truth in the traditional belief that churches were
occasionally used for secular purposes such as parish feasts, church ales,
or similar merry-making. But very little firm documentary evidence
survives concerning such uses, and in the absence of any such evidence
the question of whether it was a *normal* or *common* late medieval practice
to hold church ales or other secular activities in the naves of parish churches
must remain in doubt. In this connection an entry which occurs in several
late medieval churchwardens' accounts has given rise to considerable
misunderstanding. This concerns references to 'the Dance of Powles' or
'Dance of Pauls'. For example the accounts of St Edmund's Salisbury for
1490–91 contain the following entries:

1490	To Willm Belrynger for clensinge of the Churche at ye Dawnse of Powles	8d
1491	For a pece of Tymber for a ynner grounselle of Powlis Daunce	3s 1d
	To Will Joynour for workmanship of the seid Powlis Daunce	10s 2d
	To John Lokyar for xxxiiii grete nailes for the Daunce of Powlis	4d

Similar entries can be found in the churchwardens' accounts of some of the
Bristol churches and elsewhere, and it has been suggested that they refer
to dancing in the church, perhaps by children around a maypole. In fact
these entries refer to hanging up a painting on canvas depicting the Dance
of Death or the *Danse Macabre*. This morbid subject was very popular
in the late Middle Ages, and showed the figure of Death as a dancing
skeleton inviting various classes of contemporary society to join him.

An early and very famous example of this painting was displayed in St
Paul's cathedral and for this reason the subject became known as the
'Dance of Pauls'.

Even though the surviving evidence is not copious, enough remains to show that feasts were certainly held in some churches. Church ales have already been mentioned, and weddings, baptisms and funerals were also occasionally accompanied by feasting and drinking in the church. The will of Margaret Atkinson dated 18 October 1544 gives explicit details of a memorial feast:

The Sunday next after her burial, there shall be provided two dozens of bread, a kilderkin of ale, two gammons of bacon, three shoulders of mutton, and two couples of rabbits, desiring all the parish, as well rich as poor, to take part thereof, and a table to be set in the middle of the church with everything necessary thereunto.

But although such documentary evidence is sparse, there is no lack of information about the secular rise of churchyards. Before the custom of erecting elaborate gravestones became common, churchyards were unencumbered with obstructions and were admirably suited to all sorts of recreational use. For example, in 1332 the bishop ordered that fairs should no longer be held in and around the cathedral at Wells, but little notice was taken and they continued to be held both there and at nearby St Cuthbert's. At Shaftesbury in 1311 the bishop ordered that rough games in the churchyard should stop, and that animals should not be allowed to graze among the graves, but it is clear that it was only *rough* games which might lead to disorder or even bloodshed that were prohibited. The sort of problem which could arise, and illustrating the sort of use to which churchyards could be put, is shown in an incident at Beckington in Somerset in 1498. George Hammond and John Taylor appeared before the Bishop's court at Wells and confessed that they, with others, had played ball in the churchyard at Beckington 'and that they had fought with one another even to the shedding of blood'. They were ordered to do penance in the church on three successive Sundays. At Dundry on the steep hillside overlooking the port of Bristol there are references to a maypole being erected annually in the churchyard, and of all sorts of games taking place around the church there—wrestling, dancing, cudgels, fives, and other sports. Bishop Grosseteste of Lincoln condemned in 1236 the practice of holding markets and fairs in churchyards, and rough games such as tilting at a quintain on a wheel.

At Yeovil in Somerset the churchwardens derived a large part of their income during the later Middle Ages from the stall-keepers at the weekly market in the little town who paid to be allowed to erect their booths against the churchyard wall, and also from those who rented the weights and measures which were kept in the parish church. St Edmund's church at Salisbury had a regular income from stall-holders who rented standings both in the churchyard and along the churchyard wall. For example in 1491 the accounts record:

> Received of dyvers men cheese sellers which stode
> at the Walle   1s 4d

and in 1511 there were receipts from stall-holders and cheese-sellers:

> infra interiorem partem et exteriorem muri
> lapidis Cimiterii ecclesia predicte   3s 8½d

At Sherborne one of the market stalls actually used a buttress of All Hallows, the parish church, as a counter. The church house at Ashburton (Devon) as well as the space in front of it were used during the fifteenth century for stalls which were let out on fair and market days and provided a regular source of income for the churchwardens. The churchwardens of St Lawrence, Reading, received an income for standings erected in the churchyard and even in the church porch during the annual fair, and during the fifteenth century there were complaints from the churchwardens of St Michael-le-Belfry, York, about the noise and disturbance caused by buying and selling at markets in the churchyard, while at Rickall in Yorkshire the churchwardens complained in 1519 that 'pedlars come on festival days into the porch of the church and there sell their wares'.

Plays and performances by minstrels were also common in churches and churchyards during the late Middle Ages. In 1451 a play called 'Christmasse Play' brought a profit of 6s 8d to the churchwardens at Tintinhull (Somerset), and the churchwardens at St Michael's, Bath staged a play in the church there in 1482. At Ashburton (Devon) the churchwardens' accounts show occasional payments to visiting bearwards, who no doubt were thus rewarded for bringing their animals to lend further spectacle to the parish church ale; and there were frequent payments to players for the performance of stage plays at the church ales. The Ashburton churchwardens also kept a stock of players' clothes and other stage properties, which they often lent out to neighbouring parishes, and which a local tailor was occasionally employed to repair. As well as costumes, the Ashburton collection also included devils' heads, rattlebags for the devils, wigs, staves, crests and gloves. At Ashburton the plays were undoubtedly performed inside the church, since there are references to 'the pleers of a Cryssmas game that pleyed yn the churche'. In 1479 the churchwardens of St John's, Peterborough, paid 1s 8d to actors who performed a Christmas play in the church. Many fifteenth-century churchwardens' accounts from all over the country contain similar entries of income from plays performed either in the church or churchyard, or of expenses incurred in hiring costumes and properties for the players. There can be no doubt that such religious plays and spectacles were very common and were also extremely popular. The churchwardens' accounts of Yatton in Avon record regular payments to minstrels for playing in the church. There was a regular gild of minstrels attached to the church of St Mary Magdalene at Launceston which Bishop Lacy in 1440 encouraged the faithful to support with their alms; and in 1478 it was stated that the Mayor and burgesses of Launceston had long been accustomed to hire singing men for the church choir. The Bodmin churchwardens received the sum of 5s 0d towards their fund for rebuilding the church in 1470 from 'the players yn the Church Hay [i.e. the churchyard] William Mason and his fellowis'; while at Barnstaple in 1549 the churchwardens 'paied to the players that played at Church 2s 8d'. The great Cornish cycle of miracle plays, although generally enacted in the open air, were nonetheless essentially connected with the parish churches and their teaching. The Cornish plays were also great popular occasions, providing a dramatic spectacle as well as religious teaching. Richard Carew in *c* 1600 commented on the popularity of these plays in Cornwall, and wrote that 'The country people flock from all sides, many miles off, to hear and see it, for they have therein devils and devices to delight as well the eye as the ear'. In the same way the famous plays and pageants of towns such as Coventry and York provided a great attraction for the spectators who flocked for miles to see them. Many of these dramatic productions contained much that was secular and even profane material with coarse humour and buffoonery, as well as their central story, and they were designed to appeal to a mass audience of illiterate or semi-literate people.

Minstrels also performed in the parish churches, and there are many references in late medieval churchwardens' accounts to various musical as well as dramatic performances. At Cirencester in Gloucestershire the church has several gargoyles evidently intended to represent revellers at a Whitsun ale; many of them bear musical instruments, and one has carved upon it the exhortation 'Be Merry'. One interesting effect of dramatic performances may be seen on the western face of the fifteenth-century tower of Bruton in Somerset, where the carver had depicted the Risen Christ surrounded by angels carrying the instruments of the Passion—

hammer, ladder, crown of thorns, scourge, etc. This common subject in late medieval iconography would be unremarkable except that the angels are shown with feathered legs. It seems highly probable that the carver was copying the angels he had seen in mystery plays wearing a costume of feathers. Angels which are also obviously copied from dramatic representations can also be seen depicted in the fifteenth-century stained glass at Lydiard Tregoze in Wiltshire. In many places the characters of Robin Hood, Little John, Maid Marion and others were depicted in summer plays and revels, and these, like Hock-tide* and May Day celebrations, were commonly held in the churchyards and contributed revenue to the parish churches. For example at Croscombe in Somerset the 'Robin Hode money' was an important source of income for the churchwardens during the sixteenth century; and at Yeovil 'Robin Hood' or 'Robert Hood' as he is sometimes described, made an annual collection from the townspeople, and in 1519 the churchwardens noted that they had 'Received of Richard Hacker this year being Robyn Hood that by his good persuasyon and dylygent labours, and by the good donacion of the towne and the countrey he presented to God and holy church £6 os 8½d'. At Weymouth during the early sixteenth century the persons who played the parts of Robin Hood and Little John were so vigorous in their collection of money from the citizens, and so violent against those who they considered not to have contributed sufficiently freely, that there were numerous complaints about their activities, and some prominent, outraged citizens even alleged that they had been pushed into the harbour through the excessive enthusiasm of Robin Hood and his fellows. The parish of Mere in Wiltshire had an annual ceremony at the church ale which involved a Cuckoo King and Cuckoo Prince, who were chosen each year from among the young men of the parish; and each year also a barrel of gunpowder was purchased by the churchwardens and was apparently used to make fireworks which were let off during the Cuckoo ceremonies.

The regular round of processions and celebrations which marked the passage of the year was also intimately associated with the parish church. The processions such as those on Palm Sunday, Corpus Christi and Rogationtide were obviously religious in purpose, though often accompanied with considerable horse-play and merry-making. But events which were essentially non-religious or even pre-Christian in origin also came within the sphere of influence of the church and churchwardens in most

* Hock-tide was the second Monday and Tuesday after Easter.

country parishes and contributed money to the church coffers. Such events varied widely in different parts of the country, but they included well-dressing, rush-strewing, the feast of fools on the feast of the Circumcision, carolling and wassailing, Plough Monday* ceremonies and dancing and other revels at Hock-tide.

An important part in the religious and social life of many parishes was played by the gilds or societies that flourished so abundantly in late medieval England. The gilds were charitable, fraternal and religious in purpose, many were dedicated to a patron saint, others were for those engaged in particular trades or occupations. For example in the Somerset village of Croscombe during the fifteenth century there were gilds of the Young Men, the Maidens, the Weavers, the Fullers, the Archers, the Hogglers (probably labourers) and the Wives. At Bodmin during the fifteenth century there were nearly 40 different gilds, including such trade gilds as St Petrock for skinners and glovers, St Dunstan and St Eloy for smiths and farriers, St Anian for shoemakers, St Martin for millers, and St John the Baptist for drapers and tailors. The little parish of Menheniot in Cornwall had gilds of St Anne, St John, St Christopher, St Nicholas, St Lallowe and St John the Baptist; each gild collected money for its own altars, and for the maintenance of the church and its ornaments; a few also traded in wool and sheep as a means of increasing the wealth which they could lavish on the parish church. Civic and gild ceremonies alike were intimately bound up with the services of the parish church, and illustrate clearly the pervasive role of religion in pre-Reformation life. A formal procession to church and a corporate act of worship were essential parts of the annual ceremonies of craft gilds, and in towns such civic functions as the annual mayoral oath-taking ceremony were conducted in the parish church. Before the Reformation regular, formal church attendance, even daily attendance, was expected of the mayor and the city fathers in towns such as York, Coventry, Norwich and Bristol. The gilds also performed an important function in late medieval communities by organising and participating in such events and spectacles as the Rogationtide, Ascension, Whitsun and Corpus Christi processions and the plays, pageants, bonfires, 'drinkings' and other celebrations of Palm Sunday, Eastertide, Midsummer, Michaelmas and Christmas. These annual rituals, processions, miracle-plays and the like all helped to preserve the integrated fabric of medieval community life, and the fact that so much of

---

* Plough Monday was the first Monday after the Epiphany.

the social and religious ritual perished or was unrecognisably altered during the Reformation vastly impoverished communal life in town and country parishes alike.

Most gilds also contributed generously to their parish churches both in money and gifts and in some places undertook the building or rebuilding of a whole aisle or sometimes even of the whole church. Some gilds also had chantries where regular masses were said for the souls of the departed members; others also had schools, often for the education of members' children and sometimes kept by the chantry priest. Bishop Stapledon of Exeter founded a school at Ashburton in 1314, and his successor Bishop Grandisson established one at Ottery St Mary. There were medieval schools at Sherborne, Wimborne and Gillingham in Dorset; and many of the monastic foundations had schools attached to them like the school at Crantock in Cornwall which was run by the college of secular canons there.

Since they were generally the only large buildings in the parish, churches were often used for secular meetings, and for manorial and other courts. Such use is admirably summed up by a sixteenth-century witness in a Star Chamber case concerning lands in Lincolnshire—

... out of time of remembrance of many their within the said parish hathe been accustomed that whensoever any thing or act was to be entreated or concluded for the benefit as well of the church of Holbeach aforesaid or for the amendment of the sea dykes and bankes within the same towns or for any other cause or matter concerning the wealthe of the saide towne it hathe been used by them all the said tyme because the paryshe there ys gret and the parishioners also dwelling wyde a sondre that a bell within the said churche hathe beene used to be knolled or rungen to the entent that the said parish heryng the said bell should resort thither to comon and to entreat of and uppon such cause ...

Manorial courts were also held in churches, and continued to be held in the churches of Alrewas and Yoxall in Staffordshire until the nineteenth century. Agreements also continued to be made and disputes settled in churches until comparatively recent times.

THE CHURCH HOUSE

A most important development affecting parish churches and community life during the later Middle Ages was the establishment of church houses. These were buildings either specifically constructed or adapted for use as parish meeting-houses, and by 1500 many parishes possessed a church house. They were especially common in south-west England, where many of the buildings survive, though few continue to be used for parish meetings and recreation. As soon as a parish had a church house, church ales and parish gatherings of all sorts could from thenceforth be held in the church house and the nave of the church, no longer needed for such events, could acquire seats and pews. In 1445 for example, the church-wardens at Yatton (Avon) collected money and paid for the building of a church house, which from then on was used for all sorts of fund-raising activities for the church. A list of the contents of the Yatton church house made a few years later shows that it contained the following:

A chettyll (kettle)	2 kyve vates
2 grett crocks	2 trowys (troughs)
2 lyttl crocks	9 stands
4 pannys	barrellys
a botum for a panne	21 trandyllys (trendles)
a brandyce	6 borde cloths (table cloths)
5 tun vats	

Typical of many church houses is that at Long Ashton (Avon). It was built near the church during the later fifteenth century and was used for parish meetings, revels, feasts and other communal events. It was known as The Angel. During the seventeenth century it ceased to be used as a church house and became an alehouse and it survives today as a public house, still called by its original name, *The Angel*. In the nearby village of Chew Magna (Avon) the church house was built in 1519 and continued in use until the mid-seventeenth century. It then became in turn a dwelling-house, the parish poor-house and a school. In the twentieth century it has been restored to its original use as a parish meeting-hall.

From their establishment during the fifteenth century until the Puritan fervour of the seventeenth century put an end to their activities, the church houses were the focus of the social life of the parish. Generally they were situated beside or near the churchyard, and many are still easily recognis-able. They were equipped with a kitchen and utensils as well as with a large meeting-room, so that in many places they were in great demand for wedding feasts as well as for parochial events.

Much of the traditional merry-making which was associated with parish churches was brought to an end by the Reformation, and more particularly by the growth of Puritan feeling during the late sixteenth and early seventeenth centuries. The effects of these changes both on the appearance of parish churches and on the part they played in community life will be discussed in the following chapter.

4. The effects of the Reformation

When the Reformation Parliament was summoned by Henry VIII and began its meetings on 3 November 1529, few could have imagined the sweeping changes in religion and religious institutions which the next three decades were to witness. By 1540 the wealthy and powerful religious houses with their large estates and magnificent buildings, which had dominated the landscape of town and country alike, had ceased to exist and there were no more monks or nuns. Soon afterwards the chantries and religious gilds were abolished, the Latin mass brought to an end, and the Catholic church, which a few years before had seemed so powerful and which was so intimately involved in all aspects of national life, had become an illegal and persecuted organisation. These massive changes were accompanied by radical alterations to the interior appearance and services of English parish churches. One of the most interesting features of the religious changes of the sixteenth century is the way in which, with few exceptions, churchwardens and congregations accommodated themselves to every development in religious policy which followed the accession of each new monarch, and without any apparent protest obeyed each new government edict. Thus screens, images, vestments and other ornaments of the churches were removed during the reign of Edward VI, replaced under Mary and abandoned again under Elizabeth with a remarkable absence in most parishes of strongly expressed feeling. There is little evidence as to whether the contradictory orders of each new government were obeyed willingly or grudgingly by the parishes, whether the changes were welcomed or resented, whether there was any regret at the loss of so many things of great beauty and value or indignation at the expense involved. All that can be said with certainty is that in most parishes the instructions of successive governments were for the most part carried out immediately and without public protest. This chapter will examine the course of these changes and the effects which they had upon the furnishings, decoration and appearance of English parish churches, and, in so far as this can be determined, upon the attitude of the parishioners towards the Church and its services.

The early changes of the Reformation—the break with Rome, the elevation of the monarchy to the position of Supreme Head of the Church, the dissolution of the monasteries and the confiscation by the Crown of all their property—had little effect upon the parish churches. The first change which affected the ordinary parishioner came with the Royal Injunctions of 1538 which ordered, among other things, that registers of baptisms, marriages and burials should be kept in every parish and that an English bible should be provided in every church—'one book of the whole Bible of the largest volume in English, and the same set up in some convenient place within the said church that you have cure of, whereas your parishioners may most commodiously resort to the same and read it.' In many parishes the registers, or later copies of them, survive from 1538, and churchwardens' accounts not infrequently record the purchase of a 'sure coffer' to contain the registers as ordered by the Injunctions. Church-wardens' accounts from all over the country also reveal that the order concerning a bible in English was obeyed immediately; for example at All Saints' Bristol in 1538 the churchwardens purchased an English bible for 16s od and 'a boke for wrytt yn al christenynge, weddyng and beryng' for 1s 8d, while at Houghton Conquest in Bedfordshire the churchwardens paid £1 4s od 'for a Bible when the parish were commanded to have one in the church'. This was the 'Great Bible' which is familiar as the source of the version of the psalms in the book of Common Prayer of 1662. The Injunctions of 1538 also began the process whereby the parish churches were ruthlessly stripped of so many of their ornaments and denuded of objects which could be regarded as superstitious or idolatrous. The clergy were ordered to issue stern warnings to their congregations against 'that most detestable offence of idolatry', to remove images and pictures which might be the object of superstitious veneration, and to warn their people that

images serve for none other purpose but as to be books of unlearned men that cannot know letters, whereby they might be otherwise admonished of the lives and conversation of them that the said images do represent; which images if they abuse for any other intent than for such remembrances, they commit idolatry in the same to the great danger of their souls. . . .

This resulted in the removal of some images and pictures, but for the most part the traditional ceremonies and services continued unchanged during the reign of Henry VIII, and the interior appearance of most parish churches was little altered. It was during the six years of the reign of Edward VI (1547–53) that the really sweeping changes occurred. These started in 1547 with the dissolution of the chantries. A chantry was an endowment whereby a priest was employed to say masses for the soul of the founder or founders of the chantry and for the souls of all the Christian departed. The founding of chantries by individuals or by groups, gilds and fraternities became very popular during the later Middle Ages, and many chantries were established in side chapels, transepts, aisles or in specially built annexes. In addition there were many other smaller endowments for the provision of lights or for the saying of occasional masses. All these were dissolved and their property confiscated by the Crown in 1547. The effect upon the parish churches was not only in the loss of endowments and of the services of the chantry priests, but also they were denuded of the plate, lamps, books and vestments which had belonged to the chantries. Moreover the abolition of the chantries brought a profound change to the social, charitable and educational life of many parishes. For many of the gilds had maintained chantries, and no longer were there to be gild processions through the streets and convivial dinners to mark the festival of the gild's patron saint, no more 'drinkings' or 'cakes and ale' on the eves of the greater feasts, no more ceremonial readings of the benefactors' names and solemn prayers for the departed, and no more mutual charity and help in times of need for members of the parish gilds. Some chantries had also been responsible for the upkeep of roads and bridges, as at Bristol where the chantry on the bridge was charged with the duty 'to keep and repair the Bridge of Bristol, piers, arches and walls, for the defence thereof against the ravages of the sea ebbing and flowing daily under the same'. Other chantries distributed alms or food to the poor, and some maintained schools such as the Gild of the Holy Cross in Birmingham whose chantry school was later to be refounded as the school of King Edward VI, or the little chantry at Houghton Regis in Bedfordshire where the chantry priest taught 6 poor children; his teaching was better than nothing although at the time when his chantry was swept away he was described as 'meanly learned'. In contrast the chantry school at Week St Mary in Cornwall was famous throughout Devon and Cornwall for its high standards, and many of the sons of the gentry were educated there. In the same year that the chantries were abolished, 1547, a further series of royal Injunctions were issued which carried further the warnings already issued about images and objects of superstitious reverence. The clergy were ordered to 'take away, utterly extinct, and destroy' all shrines, candlesticks and pictures, and 'all other monuments of feigned miracles, pilgrimages, idolatry and superstition', and to warn their parishioners against the dangers of all these things. These Injunctions signalled the start of a great wave of destruction which during the next few years was to transform the interior appearance of English parish churches. Churchwardens' accounts from all over the country bear witness to this destruction. At St Ewen's in Bristol during 1548 the tabernacles, images and the great rood—the figure of the crucified Christ with its attendant figures of the Blessed Virgin and St John—were all taken down, the candlesticks and the painted canvas screens and cloths used to decorate the rood-screen were sold, and workmen were paid 10d for 'takeinge down the tabernacles with the Images' and were given a further 1s 4d for 'takinge down the Roode and the reste of the Images', while a mason was paid 1s 6d for 'dressing upp the walls by the hye Alter'—in other words for repairing the scars left by the removal of the statues. At St Margaret's Westminster, in 1547 a large cloth painted with the Ten Commandments was bought to hang in place of the Rood; at St Martins, Leicester, in 1547 three men were paid 18d for taking down the rood-loft; and at Ludlow images of Jesus, St George, St Margaret, St Katherine and St Anne were all torn down. Similar examples of demolition can be multiplied from wherever churchwardens' accounts survive to bear witness to the destruction. It required only one determined man in a parish to destroy much of great beauty and value within a church—like one Forde, who was a master at Winchester College during the later years of Henry VIII, and who objected to the statues in the college chapel as being idolatrous. One night, therefore, he 'tyed a longe coorde to the images, lynkyng them all in one coorde, and being in his chamber after midnight, he plucked the cordes ende, and at one pulle all the golden godes came downe with *heyho Rombelo*'. A further period of devastation in the furnishings of English parish churches followed the passage through Parliament in 1550 of the 'Act against Superstitious Books and Images', and orders concerning the destruction of stone altars in churches and their replacement by wooden communion-tables. Surviving inventories of the goods which English parish churches possessed just before the Reformation reveal a large number of service books of all kinds, missals, antiphoners, festivals, books of chants and psalters. Many of these were manuscript productions of great beauty and often were elaborately decorated; the few survivals like the Antiphoner from Ranworth in Norfolk are a constant reminder of the superb beauty and exquisite workmanship of many of these books. Most were ruthlessly destroyed as a result of the legislation of 1550, as at North Elmham in Norfolk where the churchwardens disposed of 'ye gret Antyphoners, Grayles, Legends, Masbokes, and all other Kynds of boks of ye old service'. Throughout the country the solidly-built stone altars were laboriously hacked out and destroyed and were replaced by wooden communion-tables. At St Stephen's Walbrook the wardens paid 7s 6d to '5 laborers for 3 dayes at 6d at the pullyng downe of the awters': at All Saints in Bristol the churchwardens paid 4s 4d 'for Whit lymynge where the Roode lofte stode and for stoping the holis (holes) and for brekyng downe the naltars [altars] and for paving where they stood', and as a result of their labours 21 loads of stone and rubble were taken out of the church, and the street-cleaner (the Raker) was paid 8d 'for carrying away ye Dust'. According to the churchwardens' accounts of Ludlow for 1551 it took two workmen six days to demolish the stone altars and four labourers 18 days to clear the church of stone, debris and dust. The whole operation cost the parish 16 shillings; a further 7 shillings and 6d had then to be spent on paying Richard Kerver to make a new wooden communion-table. The paintings with which everywhere the walls and pillars of parish churches were adorned, pictures of the saints, stories from the life of Our Lord and of the Virgin, apostles and martyrs, were likewise destroyed or obliterated with whitewash, thus totally changing the interior appearance of the churches. At Wing in Buckinghamshire, 5s 5d was paid 'for whyt lymyng of the church', and covering the paintings; later the blank, white walls were decorated with scriptural texts. The images of the saints in the stained-glass windows also suffered great damage during the reign of Edward VI, although here the process of destruction was slower, for common sense forbade the smashing of large expanses of glass until clear glass was ready as a replacement, since otherwise many churches would have been unusuable. Gradually however during the reign of Edward and later of Elizabeth most were dismantled and destroyed. It is not always easy from the standpoint of the twentieth century to appreciate just how great the impact of these sweeping changes in the traditional furnishings and decoration of the churches and the alteration in the language and pattern of the services must have been for rural communities of the sixteenth century. Pre-reformation religion was above all a matter of form and ritual; particular ceremonies performed in a certain manner and ordered by a regular calendar of feasts and fasts. The majestic symbolism of the Mass and the colourful pageantry of the other

12. *Heckington, Lincolnshire* The elaborately carved Easter Sepulchre which is situated on the north side of the Chancel. Note the figures of the Risen Christ, the women at the tomb, and the sleeping soldiers below.

13. *Clayton, Sussex* Wall-painting over the chancel arch, showing the figure of Christ seated in judgement.

14. *Pickering, North Yorkshire* Restored fifteenth-century wall-painting of St George and the Dragon

services of the church were deeply embedded in the traditional life of men and women. The annual round of ceremonies and processions, the joyous celebrations of Christmas and Easter, the sombre call to repentance of Lent and the solemn mourning of Holy Week, candles at Candlemas, ashes on Ash Wednesday, palms on Palm Sunday, creeping to the Cross on Good Friday, the Easter Sepulchre, the Corpus Christi processions, the patronal festivals—all these and many others gave form and order to secular and religious life. In a few brief years all were either swept away or totally altered, and the disturbance for individual as well as for community religious life must have been even greater than is apparent from the surviving documentary evidence. Latin Mass was replaced by services in English, the Prayer Book of 1549 was the first book of *common* prayer, i.e. to be used in the same form throughout the whole country, without the regional variations and uses which had developed in the Mass over the centuries. This was followed in 1552 by the second Book of Common Prayer, more protestant in its theology than the first. Again, the church-wardens' accounts bear witness to the purchase of these books in conformity with the edicts of the government. For example at Melton Mowbray in 1549, 6s 0d was spent 'for a book of the nue survice'; and at St Mary's Dover they spent 6s 8d 'for a new boke of the service of the Churche caulid the Communyon boke'. The use of the English language for the services must have seemed another enormous and bewildering change to the laity, emphasising the magnitude of the revolution, though there are few references to the way in which it was received. The extent of feeling engendered in the twentieth century by comparatively minor alterations in the liturgy of the church of England, and by changes in the traditional services and the 'externals' of Anglican worship, or the disquiet felt by many contemporary Catholics over the use of English for the Mass, is sufficient to remind us of the disturbance and unease which must have been caused by the major changes which were witnessed by sixteenth-century congregations. In time, the solemn dignity of Archbishop Cranmer's Book of Common Prayer gained it acceptance and accorded it a lasting impact upon the speech patterns of Englishmen. The strongest immediate reaction to the English services came from Devon and Cornwall, with the so-called Prayer Book Rebellion of 1549. There were various underlying causes of this short-lived revolt, economic and social as well as religious, but it was the English Prayer Book which sparked it off. Particularly this was so in Cornwall where the English language was as alien as the Latin of the Mass and lacked even the virtue of tradition and familiarity. The Cornish rebels of 1549 described the new Prayer Book as 'but like a Christmas game . . . . and so we Cornish men (whereof certain of us understand no English) utterly refuse this new English'. Archbishop Cranmer, evidently stung by the Cornishmen's contemptuous rejection of the Prayer Book on which he had expended so much labour, could not resist a reply, inquiring how many of them understood the Latin of the Mass. From Cornwall also we get a rare glimpse of the impact of the religious changes upon everyday life. Richard Carew, the sixteenth-century Cornish historian, recorded that during 1548-49 the boys at Bodmin school were split into two parties, 'the one whereof they called the old religion, the other the new'. Fierce fights took place between each side which culminated in one of the boys making a gun out of an old candlestick; he 'charged it with powder and stone and . . . . therewith killed a calf: whereupon the owner complained, the master whipped, and the division ended'. Unfortunately, the divisions in the country at large were not so easily resolved. In 1552 English parish churches were at the further expense of purchasing the revised Prayer Book, but this time there was even less reaction. The churchwardens of St Mary's, Devizes, for example, paid 4s 8d for 'the new Bookes of Common Prayer', and at St Mary's, Cambridge three of the new books cost 15s 4d, and the church-wardens also purchased parts of the book set to music:

Ye copy of ye servys in inglys sette oute by note	3s 4d
For wryghtynge and notyng part of yt to syng on bothe sydes of ye quyre	1s 4d

In 1551 a further assault was made on the possessions of parish churches when the Privy Council ordered that 'for as much as the Kinge's Majestie hath neede presently of a masse of mooney, therefore commissions shulde be addressed into all shires to take into the Kinge's hands suche church plate as remayneth, to be emploied unto his highness use'. This iniquitous order resulted in the looting from all parish churches of their silver chalices, patens, censers, jewels, vestments and other plate by the Crown, in each case leaving to the churches only the worst or least valuable chalice and paten for use in the Holy Communion service. Again, there are few references to any reaction in the parishes though careful study of church-wardens' accounts does reveal that a few, sensing what was afoot, had already disposed of their valuables before the King's commissioners arrived. At St Lawrence, Reading, the bulk of the church plate was sold by the churchwardens in 1547 for £47 18s 0d and some of the money was used for paving the streets. At St Martin's, Leicester, quantities of plate, ornaments and vestments were sold during Edward VI's reign, and at Yatton on the low-lying coastal plain of north Somerset the silver cross from the high altar was sold by the churchwardens in 1549 and the money used to make a barrier against tidal flooding, 'a sirten sklusse (Sluice) or yere (weir) agenste the rage of ye salte water'. In many Essex parishes during the early years of King Edward VI the images were torn down and church goods were sold so that the money could be applied to the care of the poor, education, church repairs, maintenance of roads and bridges and other good causes where it would be secure from royal confiscation. At Dovercourt (Essex) the churchwardens 'with the assent and consent of other the said inhabitants' sold a cross, chalice and censer for £21; at Rayleigh two silver-gilt basins were sold for £9 3s 0d and the money used for church repairs; the censer, ship (container for incense), two paxes and a chalice belonging to the church of Great Burstead realised £12 13s 4d and the money was divided between church repairs and the poor. Extensive sales of plate from the wealthy church of Saffron Walden brought in nearly £100 which was used for the relief of the poor, the maintenance of a free school and 'other charitable deeds'.

In 1553 the young King Edward VI died and was succeeded by his half-sister Mary. In the course of her reign Queen Mary renounced all the changes in religion and in the services and appearance of the churches which had been made during the previous two decades, and returned to the situation as it had been before Henry VIII had begun the religious upheaval. For those who had regretted or resented the changes of the reign of Edward VI it must have been a great joy to see the Latin mass and the old round of familiar feasts and saints' days restored once more. There were, however, many others who did not welcome the restoration of the old ways, and who steadfastly refused to obey the edicts of the government. The story of the martyrs of Mary's reign, of the horrific tally of burnings and persecution, is too well known to need retelling here, but what must be emphasised is that the changes which were ordered were apparently carried out in the parish churches without question or delay. With a few notable exceptions, most of those who suffered for their adherence to Protestantism under Mary were drawn from the lower orders of society, shopkeepers, tradesmen, craftsmen; the wealthier sections of the community, the leaders of society in rural parishes from whom the churchwardens were generally chosen, conformed or at least concealed any open opposition to the Marian as to all other Tudor governments. No hostile reaction was apparently provoked even though the restorations of Mary's reign cost the parishes a great deal of money. For whereas the destruction of furnishings and decorations under Edward had not involved much expenditure, the replacement of rood-screens, vestments, stone altars, plate, Latin service books, censers and other necessary equipment under Mary was extremely expensive. But again churchwardens' accounts from all over the country show that parish churches were rapidly re-equipped with all the things necessary for the conduct of the services in the Catholic tradition, the stone altars were rebuilt, the rood-screens and their figures replaced, and new vestments, service books, candlesticks, censers, containers for holy oil and images of the saints were purchased. The wardens at St James', Garlickhythe in London paid £4 13s 8d for a new Rood and a new Easter Sepulchre to replace those torn out only a few years before; at Stamford in Berkshire some idea that the restoration of the old order was welcomed comes through the accounts, for a new stone altar was built and the wooden communion-table 'which served in ye churche for ye communion in the wycked tyme of sysme [schism]' was sold for 5s 0d. The sentences of scripture were removed from the walls of churches and a start was made upon restoring the old decorations, pictures of the saints, statues and stained glass. But the five years of Mary's reign ended with her death in November 1558, and Elizabeth's accession and subsequent decision to restore the religious legislation of her father's later years, the break with Rome and the position of the church of England, led to a further orgy of destruction. Roods, statues, screens, vestments, stone altars and Latin service books were once more swept away, and wooden communion-tables, English bibles and service books and walls adorned with biblical texts were restored. Commissioners toured the country to see that the work of destruction was carried out, and few rood-screens or stone altars survived their visits. The following extracts from the wardens' accounts of St Mary's, Devizes covering the decade 1551–1561 tell their own tale of the bewildering rapidity of change in the church:

1551 (Ed. VI)	Paid for . . . plucking down of the (stone) Altars	1s 2d
1553 (Mary)	Paid for . . . setting up the great Altar . .	8d
1555 (Mary)	Paid for defacing the Scriptures on the Walls .	2s 4d
	Paid for . . . putting in the Roodloft . .	6s 0d
1557 (Mary)	Paid for tymber to make the pyctor (picture) that standeth by the Rode named Mary and John .	2s 0d
1561 (Elizabeth)	Paid for taking down of the Roodloft . .	6s 0d

Similarly at Ashburton in Devon, 3s 4d was paid in 1549 'for takyng down the Rood and other images'; later these were all burnt. Under Mary the rood and the stone altars were restored, only to be taken down again and destroyed early in the reign of Elizabeth.

The effect of these changes in religion, both in theology and in the outward trappings, upon the attitude of parishioners to their church and its services can only have been profound, but comparatively little evidence survives to bear witness to their inner feelings. Most avoided trouble and conformed to each change without any outward sign of protest; the martyrs of each side, though unquestionably heroic and important, are nonetheless not typical. By the reign of Elizabeth, however, respect for the church and for the clergy had notably declined, and notwithstanding many notable exceptions to the contrary, the standards of the clergy in piety, learning and conscientiousness were at a low ebb. One source which does offer an opportunity of approaching the opinions of ordinary men and women about the religious changes of the time and concerning their own thoughts of the hereafter, may be found in the wills which they left. The first bequest in a sixteenth-century will was of the soul of the testator to God, and the phrases which are employed in bequeathing the soul may afford some glimpse of the religious opinions of the person making the will. This was probably the only time in his life that an ordinary person had occasion to set down on paper any hint of his religious beliefs, and wills from various parts of the country have recently been carefully studied with this in mind. The will may of course have been written by a scribe who employed a common form for this part or merely copied from some other will; but nevertheless a devout Catholic would bequeath his soul not only to God but also 'to the Blessed Virgin Mary and the whole Company of Heaven', while a Protestant testator would use a phrase such as to 'Almighty God and his only Son our Lord Jesus Christ, by whose precious death and passion I hope only to be saved'. There are many thousands of wills surviving from the sixteenth century, and it is clear from those that have so far been analysed that there was a steady growth of Protestant belief during the middle decades of the sixteenth century. For example, Professor A. G. Dickens has analysed wills from Yorkshire and Nottinghamshire and shows that whereas in the late 1530s only some 14 per cent of wills contained protestant phraseology, by the early 1550s the proportion omitting all reference to the Virgin and the saints had risen to more than 60 per cent. But whether they were Catholic or Protestant, few men during the sixteenth or seventeenth centuries doubted that God was intimately concerned with the minutest details of their daily lives. Likewise plagues, disease and natural disasters were attributed to the direct intervention of the Almighty in punishing some wickedness, just as good fortune was regarded as a sign of divine favour. A hard-headed and highly successful sixteenth-century Bristol merchant, when sending valuable cargoes abroad, was careful to note against each entry in his Ledger 'God send hit saff'; and it was more than common form that sixteenth- and seventeenth-century letter-writers ended their correspondence with phrases such as 'May God send you long life and good fortune', 'Our Lord Jesus Christ preserve you in grace', or 'I pray God to send you as well fare as your heart desireth'. Typical also of the feeling that the controlling hand of the Almighty touched every aspect of life was the Berkshire farmer, Robert Loder who, when making up his accounts for the year 1616, wrote:

> This year sowing too early I lost (The Lord being the cause thereof, but that the instrument wherewith it pleased him to work) . . . the sum of £10 at least, so exceeding full was my barley with charlock, in all likelihood by means of that instrumental cause, the Lord my God . . . being without doubt the efficient cause thereof.

THE ELIZABETHAN CHURCH

The newly-formed Church of England in the reign of Elizabeth faced a multitude of difficulties. The dissolution of the monasteries meant that the patronage and right to tithes formerly possessed by the monasteries passed into the hands of laymen (the lay rectors) and numerous parishes and vicars were thus robbed of endowments or were scandalously ill-paid. The new church with its emphasis on preaching rather than on the sacraments found that many of the clergy were insufficiently educated for this new role, and could do no more than read from the 'Homilies' issued by the Elizabethan government. Moreover, the changes of the previous decades had meant that many of the most high-principled clergy had resigned their livings or had been deprived by one party or the other, and increasing opportunities for educated laymen to find employment outside the church meant that there was a lack of suitable candidates for ordination. Many bishops found woeful inadequacies in their clergy, like Bishop Hooper of Gloucester during the reign of Edward VI, who found that several of his clergy could not recite the commandments, while the vicar of South Cerney believed that the Lord's Prayer was so called because it 'was given by his lord the King and written in the King's book of

Common Prayer'. In Lancashire during the years 1562 to 1569 Bishop
Downham ordained no fewer than 176 priests, but closer examination
reveals that there was not one graduate among them and that 56 of them
were noted as being 'tolerantia domini episcopi', in other words that they
were ordained in spite of their educational failings, presumably for want
of more suitably qualified candidates. In 1562 a Manchester curate was
ordered to attend daily at the grammar school and to learn a chapter of the
New Testament each month for examination by the bishop. Elizabethan
audiences could easily recognise and be amused by the cynical and inadequate vicar, Sir Oliver Martext, portrayed by Shakespeare in *As You Like
It*, or the Welsh figure of fun, Sir Hugh Evans, the parson in *The Merry
Wives of Windsor*. In contrast, out of countless good, learned and dedicated
men in the Elizabethan church we can cite the example of Richard Green-
ham, the incumbent of Dry Drayton in Cambridgeshire from 1570 to
1591, of whom it was said that he

spared no pains amongst his people, whereby he might advance the good of
their souls: His constant course was to preach twice on the Lord's day, and
before the evening sermon to Catechize the young people of the Parish. His
manner also was to preach on Mundayes, Tuesdayes and Wednesdayes and
on Thursdayes to catechize the youth and again on Fridayes to preach to
his people . . . besides his publick preaching and catechizing, his manner was
to walk out into the fields and to conferr with his Neighbours as they were
at plow. . . .

At the other extreme was George Dobson, the vicar of Whalley in Lancashire, of whom it was alleged in 1575 that he was 'a common drunkard,
and such an ale-knight as the like is not in our parish, and in the night
when most men be in bed at their rest then is he in the ale-house with a
company like to himself, but not one of them can match him in ale-house
tricks, for he will, when he cannot discern black from blue, dance with a
full cup on his head, far passing all the rest'.

Over the standards of the clergy, as in so many other matters concerning
the church, it is impossible to generalise, for there were certainly many
good, learned and conscientious men to be found in the Elizabethan
church, as well as near-illiterates and rogues, and it is only too easy to
high-light the exceptional and to forget the normal. Church building had
virtually come to an end with the Reformation, and reports made by
bishops and archdeacons at their visitations and by churchwardens during
the later sixteenth century show a disturbing state of neglect in some
churches, the result of all the changes and upheavals of the previous

decades; though here also it is only the exceptional which gets noted in the official records, and nothing is said of those churches where all was in good order. But at Shepreth in Cambridgeshire in 1579 the churchwardens' report reveals not only neglect but also the consequences which could follow the smashing of the stained-glass windows; they stated that 'the chancel is not repaired . . . . that lyeth more lyker a swines style than a place to hear gods word red in, and fyled with birds and owles to the great annoyance of the parishioners there in could frost rayne and snowey weather.' At Cothelstone in Somerset the chancel was said to be 'in decay insomuch that when it raineth the curate may not abide at the altar.' Similarly at Horsford, Norfolk, in 1597 the chancel was said to be ruinous 'both within and without so that it rayneth in such sorte that the Communion table cannot stand there.' Bishop Jewel of Salisbury wrote in 1562

it is a sin and shame to see so many churches so ruinous and so foully decayed in almost every corner. Suffer them not to be defiled with rain and weather, with dung of doves and owls, stares and choughs, and other filthiness, as it is foul and lamentable in many places in this country.

There was also great variation during Elizabeth's reign in the way in which the services were conducted and in the extent to which older ceremonies continued. In some parishes all the old customs and rituals that formerly marked the passing year had been ruthlessly swept away; in others, and particularly in the north of England, many survived until the Puritan reforms of the seventeenth century. Archbishop Grindall felt it worthwhile to enquire of all parishes in 1576 whether the minister or churchwardens had allowed

. . . . any lords of misrule or summer lords or ladies, or any disguised persons, or others, in Christmas or at May-Games, or any morris dancers, or at any other times, to come unreverently into the church or churchyard, and there to dance or play any unseemly parts, with scoffs, jests, wanton gestures or ribald talk, namely in the time of Common Prayer.

In 1581 the curate of Rufforth in Yorkshire was reported to his superiors because he 'did not onelye permit and suffer a Rishbearing [i.e. Rushbearing] with the churche' but also because he did himself 'daunce skip leape and hoighe gallantlye'.

Gradually, however, and in spite of its shortcomings, the Elizabethan church gained the acceptance of the majority of English people, though a steadfast group of determined Catholics, in spite of all persecution, remained outside its ministrations, while from within a vocal minority of

Puritans strove vainly to effect further Protestant reforms. The sanctions imposed by the government did much to drive congregations into conformity during the early years of Elizabeth's reign. Once there, the dignified English liturgy and the Bible in English helped the new church to grow in the esteem of congregations. In the middle years of the Queen's reign support for the Anglican church became inextricably entwined with nationalism and patriotism as the threat from Spain grew, and the remnant of the Catholic church in England found itself drawn unwillingly but inevitably into the whirlpool created by European political and religious conflict. Many among both clergy and laity lived through all the changes and upheavals which have been described in this chapter. They were able to look back in old age from the whitewashed, scraped church interiors of Elizabeth's reign, denuded of screens, statues and paintings, and to remember the same church in the days of their youth with its elaborate services, its colourful vestments, lights, incense and all the panoply of Catholic ceremonial.

Although large numbers of the parish clergy resigned or were ousted from their benefices during one or other of the changes of the sixteenth century, many others remained in their parishes, accepted each new order of service and theology and continued to minister to their congregations. A few were no doubt openly or privately cynical, or put the maintenance of their accustomed income before all else, or simply wished to avoid trouble. The best-known of all such men was vicar Aleyn of Bray in Berkshire who retained his benefice through all the changes of the sixteenth century, and in Thomas Fuller's famous account is said to have effectively silenced a critic who complained that he was prepared to accept any theological change, '. . . being taxed by one for being a turncoat and an unconstant changeling, "Not so", said he, "for I always kept my principle, which is this, to live and die the vicar of Bray" '.

Many other clergy were simply perplexed by the changes they were witnessing and by their involvement in controversies which they scarcely comprehended. Like William Herne who was the vicar of St Petrock's, Exeter, from 1528 until his death in 1566, and who continued to serve his parishioners there through all the religious changes. During the reign of Edward VI Herne had declared to his friend John Midwinter, who was Mayor of Exeter and a staunch protestant, that he would be torn apart by wild horses rather than say Mass again. Nevertheless, when Edward VI died and Mary came to the throne, Herne conformed to the catholic order once more. When Midwinter saw him robed for Mass he 'poynted unto him with his fynger remembringe as it were his old protestations that he would never singe masse agayne; but parson Herne openly yn the churche spak alowd unto hym. "It is no remedye man, it is no remedye".' Another example of an incumbent who although very reluctant, and much disturbed in his conscience, eventually conformed to all the changes, is Robert Parkyn who was curate of Adwick-le-Street near Doncaster (Yorkshire) during the middle years of the sixteenth century. His 'commonplace book' compiled about 1555 gives an intimate glimpse of the feelings of a conservatively-minded north-countryman who conformed with great reluctance to the changes of Edward VI's reign and rejoiced when Catholicism was restored under 'the gratius Quene Marie'. Parkyn, however, continued to hold his benefice in spite of his misgivings until his death in 1570.

Two further examples, one a priest the other a layman, will suffice to illustrate the completeness of the revolution through which such men had lived. The first is John Chetmill who was ordained as a priest early in the 1520s. In 1538 he became vicar of Sherborne, Dorset, and the parish priest of the church of All Hallows which was actually built up against the walls of the great Benedictine Abbey of St Mary's. Here he must have been quite overshadowed in every sense by the wealthy and ancient abbey with its extensive landed estates and superb church under its powerful abbot, 16 monks and numerous servants and retainers. In 1539 the monastery was suppressed and the abbot and monks departed; a year later the town acquired the great abbey church as its parish church and All Hallows was demolished. It must have been almost overwhelming for John Chetmill to find himself in charge of this enormous church with its outstanding architectural features; but he apparently accepted this change as he accepted the new English service books, the changes in the vestments and ritual and the new theology of Edward VI's reign—and as he also came to terms with the reversal of all these changes under Mary when once more he said the Latin mass and observed all the old feasts and fasts. Likewise in 1558–59 Chetmill accepted the new regime imposed by the Elizabethan government, and he remained as vicar of Sherborne until his death in 1566. It would be quite wrong to think of such a man necessarily as a turncoat or time-server. John Chetmill was evidently concerned for the well-being of his people and there is ample evidence of his dedicated work amongst them. For example, there are few wills made in the town during his incumbency which do not bear either his handwriting as the scribe or his signature as a witness, evidence of his regular attendance upon the sick and dying. It is difficult to believe that he would have served their interests better by resignation.

The second example is a layman, Roger Martyn of Long Melford in Suffolk, who has been referred to earlier. He recalled that the high altar had been dismantled under Edward VI, set up again in Queen Mary's time and finally demolished early in Elizabeth's reign. He recollected the 'rich Copes and suits of vestments', the Easter Sepulchre and the organs upon the rood-loft. These organs had been brought into his house, and he obviously kept them to await a further change in religious fashion when they might be required once more. Three times a year the choir had dined at Melford Hall, and

on St James' Even there was a bonefire and a tub of ale and bread given to the poor, and before my doore there were made three other bonfires, viz. on Midsummer Even, on the Even of St Peter and Paul when they had the like drinkings, and on St Thomas' Even, on which, if it fell not on the fish day, they had some long pyes of mutton and peasecods set out upon boards with the aforsaid quantity of bread and ale; . . . and my Grandfather . . . had, at the lighting of the bonefires, wax tapers with balls of wax, yellow and green, set up all the Breadth of the Hall, lighted them and burning there, before the image of St John the Baptist; and after they were put out, a watch candle was lighted and sit in the midst of the said Hall, upon the pavement burning all night.

The memories flow out with all the freshness and jumbled recollection of an old man recalling his youth; but through it comes the realisation that the world he remembers has disappeared. The differences which he described in the appearance of the church, the services, the ceremonies and the doctrine are a measure of the total revolution is parochial life which men like Roger Martyn and John Chetmill had witnessed in their lifetimes.

5. Parish life in the seventeenth century

In spite of the manifold changes which the sixteenth century had witnessed in the services, furnishings and appearance of English parish churches, they nevertheless continued throughout the seventeenth century to dominate the social as well as the religious life of the majority of parishioners. Perhaps the most striking of all the differences between the life and activity which centred around the pre-Reformation parish churches and the part which they played in community life after the Elizabethan Settlement is the changed attitude of the parishioners towards the church buildings. Before the Reformation parishioners eagerly lavished money on the fabric, furnishings and decoration of their churches, and as was shown in previous chapters, the constant stream of bequests and gifts from parishioners is a major feature of all pre-Reformation churchwardens' accounts. After the Reformation such gifts practically cease. Churchwardens were obliged to obtain money from compulsory church rates or from pew-rents and other charges upon church-goers. Church-building virtually ceased, and the whitewashed church interiors of Anglican seemliness, decency and order no longer attracted the generous donations of the laity. Churchwardens were constantly concerned in a struggle to secure enough money to maintain the fabric and provide the essentials for the services.

The Sunday services were, however, the only regular occasions on which the whole parish met together, and were accordingly important in the life of the community. Attendance was compulsory, and the churchwardens were charged with the duty of reporting regular absentees at the archdeacon's or bishop's visitations. The Elizabethan Act of Uniformity of 1559, which had ordered that the clergy should, under pain of severe penalties, use the Book of Common Prayer 'and none other or otherwise' in the services, also laid down that 'all and every person and persons inhabiting within this realm' should regularly attend their parish church 'upon Sunday and other days ordained and used to be kept as Holy Days, and then and there to abide orderly and soberly during the time of the Common prayer, preachings, or other service of God there to be used and ministered.' Failure to attend was to be punished by the church courts. How far regular attendance was enforced throughout the seventeenth century is not easy to tell from the records. Certainly there were occasional campaigns against non-attenders by archdeacons and bishops, and there is no doubt that attendance by everyone was the ideal. In very large parishes or in towns and among the poor classes of the community enforcement was always very difficult. Few churchwardens, however, were as blunt as those of Christchurch, Bristol in 1675, who presented a list of those who did not regularly attend church or receive the sacrament to the bishop, but noted that there were 'severall others very inconsiderable people which we thought fit purposely to omit by reason of their poverty.' Perhaps because they were obliged to attend, the behaviour of the congregations during the services was not always exemplary. William Hills of Holton St Mary, Suffolk, was accused in 1597 of having 'used in the tyme of devine service open and Rowde speeches to the disturbance of the minster'; and at Carlton in Lindrick, Nottinghamshire, in 1620 the churchwardens reported that 'the wife of George Minall of Carlton broughte a most unquiet childe to the churche to the greate offence of the whole congregation, who althoughe she was intreated by Mr Benson to sende awaye the childe yeete she would not do, so that he was enforced to give over prayers because he coulde not be hearde for the offensive noyce'. Even George Herbert, the saintly rector of Bemerton in Wiltshire during the 1630s had to exhort his congregation to attend carefully to the service and to say the responses clearly, 'not in a hudling, or slubbering fashion, gaping, or scratching the head, or spitting even in the midst of their answer'. Quarrels which had begun earlier over secular matters frequently broke out again in church when the parties found themselves in close proximity, as for example at Ryme Intrinseca, Dorset, in 1609 where it was alleged that two women of the parish continually interrupted the services with their quarrelling, 'Shusan the wief of Robert Husway and Agnes the wief of John Plowman be contendinge and sterringe in the church and the one thrustinge and pullinge out the other'. There are countless similar examples in the records of the church courts. Even more disagreeable was the conduct of Henry Spinter at Alton Pancras, Dorset, who in 1617 was drunk in church and who 'one Sabath daye a littell before the evening prayer went up into the tower and at a trappe dore did pisse

77

downe upon theare heads in the belfry that they could not stand there nor neare itt to the great offence of those that were present . . . .'. In 1637 William Allen of Earls Colne, Essex, was accused of 'pissing in the clock chamber so that it ran down and annoyed the church'.

From the fifteenth century onwards, when the practice had grown up of installing pews in parish churches, churchwardens had charged people for the right to sit in particular pews, and private pews provided a fruitful cause of dispute. In most parish churches during the seventeenth century the seating arrangements mirrored the formal social structure of the community. The parson in his often very elaborate reading-deck and pulpit, the latter with its great soundingboard and colourful, tasselled cushion very obviously the central focus of the whole assembly; the parish clerk in his own seat beneath the parson; and the squire in his large private pew; all looked down upon a congregation ranged in appropriate order. The gentry and farmers who could afford the pew-rents were accommodated in their own box pews, often so arranged that some had their backs to the altar, the labourers sat uncomfortably and closely huddled on forms at the back, while paupers and children sat on the forms in the gallery, where also the musicians were often accommodated. The church musicians and choir and the important part which they played in the church and community life will be discussed in the next chapter.

When Richard Gough of Myddle in Shropshire wrote the history of the families in his parish at the end of the seventeenth century, (the *Antiquityes and Memoryes of the Parish of Myddle*), he did so by taking each pew in the church in turn and writing about the family which occupied it, thus covering all the parishioners. To attempt to sit in a different pew in church was not therefore simply a matter of obtaining a better seat, it also altered the rigid class structure of the community. At St Mary's, Dover, in 1639 the churchwardens were authorised '. . . to place and dispose of every parishioner respectively of yor said parish in the seates of yor church according to their severall condition, qualities and estates . . .'. At Shimpling, Norfolk, in 1597 a woman was accused of creating a disturbance in the church 'by placing herself in the best pews of the parish, being placed beneath by the churchwardens'. There was a vociferous quarrel at St Ebb's, Oxford, in 1584 during service time between four women each of whom claimed the right to a certain seat, and throughout the seventeenth century the church courts heard a constant stream of cases relating to disputes and quarrels over seats in parish churches. The practice of parishioners constructing or renewing their own seats also gave rise to many complaints and objections, since often the pews were made so large and ornate that persons sitting behind could neither see nor hear the parson. The church courts heard many cases like that against Alexander Sampson of South Leverton, Nottinghamshire, in 1638 which alleged that 'he hath made a seate in our church that is not uniforme. It is higher than any other that is neare unto it, and it continues still soe high that it hideth the sight of the deske and the Alter from all them that sitt behinde itt'. A similar complaint was made to the Dean of Salisbury in 1638 by the churchwardens of Preston near Weymouth (Dorset). They complained that the pew erected by one Robert Mapp was

. . . . offensive to certayne persons sittinge behinde yt, by reason of the height of yt, yt standinge a greate deale higher than any seate in the sayd church soe that those persons there neither see nor well heare the minister reading divine service.

While it is easy to find examples of disputes and ill-behaviour during the seventeenth century, few services were enlivened by such events, and it would be wrong to suppose that in most churches the congregations behaved other than soberly and reverently. Indeed, an escape from the sheer regularity and predictability of Anglican services was one of the attractions of the multitude of dissenting bodies which grew up during the seventeenth century. It was also an important reason for absenteeism. Some absence from the Sunday services is hardly surprising when it is remembered that many parishes were very large and that people were obliged to undertake a journey of several miles in order to reach their parish church. The evidence for these long journeys is still to be seen in the multitude of hat-pegs which still adorn the walls of a few churches where they have escaped the hand of the restorer, and in the notices which survive in a few churches exhorting women to take off their pattens or over-shoes, which they wore for walking across the muddy fields, before they entered the church. The pattens were left on the stone benches which remain in so many church porches. A charming picture of people travelling a long distance to church is found in the Somerset Quarter Sessions accounts for 1627. Ellis Pawley of Martock petitioned for a renewal of his licence to sell beer at his house near the church, and his petition was supported by numerous inhabitants of the parish, who stated that

. . . . he hath a convenient clenly house for the parishioners sometimes to refresh themselves in, (they) being so far from the parish church that often times on the Sabbath day and other hollydaies they cannot go home and

79

come again to church the same day; and for that the women of the parish when they bring theire young children to be christened do often stay there to warm their babes, coming sometimes a mile, sometimes two, from home in the cold.

The excuses offered for non-attendance at church or for working on Sundays and Holy Days are many and varied. Cuthbert Atkinson of St Peter in the East, Oxford, was a fuller or cloth-worker, and in 1584 he claimed that on Sunday mornings he often had to set his cloths on the racks to dry, like most other fullers 'because otherwyse they cannot keepe promise with theire customers, for that there is sometimes scarse one fayre daye in the whole weeke'. In the same year John Collie of St Nicholas, Oxford, admitted his frequent absences from church, but stated that he was a brewer and that once he had started the brewing process he had to watch over it until it was complete, 'for whenne he doeth beginne to putt fyre under the furness he cannot departe from yt neither by day nor night untill his burden be forther . . . and by that meanes is sumwhat slacke in coming to the church'. Others had less excuse, though it seems harsh that so many farmers were brought before the church courts for tending to crops or stock either before or after services on Sundays. Some were accused simply of sitting drinking at alehouses when they should have been at church, and there are also many examples of shopkeepers and publicans being punished for opening their premises during service times. For example, an innkeeper at Saxmundham, Norfolk, in 1597 had allowed 'musitians to playe and singe and company to daunce in his house in tyme of evening prayers', while a fiddler from Sheringham in the same county was accused of playing during the service time and of drawing 'a resort of youth together to the hindrance of godly exercise'. In 1636 the wife of Edward Harris of Earls Colne, Essex, excused herself from a charge of selling beer in time of divine service by explaining that both she and her husband were at church, but 'there came one for a little beer for one that was sick, which was (sold) by a little girl that she left at home'. Generally such persons escaped with no more than an admission of guilt and a public admonition, or small fine. Continual offenders, however, risked excommunication by the church courts.

Occasionally parish-church services during the seventeenth century were enlivened by a public penance. For long after the Reformation, the church retained control of morals, and churchwardens were obliged, among their multifarious duties, to report to the church courts all lapses from moral rectitude—sexual immorality, perjury, slander, drunkenness,

15. *The Church House, Crowcombe, Somerset* This is one of the best preserved of all the church houses or parish meeting-places. It was built in 1515 and is still used by the parish.

16. *Wimborne St Giles, Dorset* The huge tomb of Sir Anthony Ashley who died in 1627. A good example of the way in which after the Reformation churches were crowded with elaborate monuments.

17. *The Sleeping Congregation, William Hogarth, 1736* A satirical portrayal of the dullness of eighteenth-century services; note the crowded pews and gallery, the royal coat of arms, hatchments, hat-pegs and the pulpit with an hour-glass for the preacher, and the parish clerk beneath.

disturbances in church and churchyard, failure to attend church or receive the communion, or other offences against ecclesiastical law. Persons reported by the churchwardens were duly tried before the church courts, and the sentences imposed ranged from excommunication and fines to public penance. Many descriptions of such public penances survive, and for the person involved it must have been an extremely daunting prospect. In a small tightly-knit local community where each person was well-known to all the others, the penitent had to appear before the whole congregation and make public confession of his or her offence. It is not too difficult to imagine the feelings of the unfortunate person compelled to undergo this punishment. At Chipping Barnet, Hertfordshire, in August 1606 Agnes Wright was ordered to undergo the ordeal of public penance, and

at the beginning of the second lesson in Morning Prayer did present herself in the middle alley of the church of Chipping Barnet, near the seat of the Minister, covered in white and there like a penitent and sorrowful sinner stood till the end of the second lesson, at which time kneeling down upon her knees she confessed that she had grievously offended Almighty God in committing fornication with one Edward Fisher of London, praying to God to forgive her and the Congregation to pray for her, that neither she nor any of them might hereafter be tempted to commit the like grievous offence. This being done she stood up again and continued until the end of Morning Prayer.

Another example, out of the many which survive, comes from an instruction sent by the Dean of Salisbury to Richard Dike, the curate of Charminster in Dorset in June 1631:

Ursula Greene of your parish is injoined on Sunday next to come to your parish church porch at the second peale to morninge prayer with a white sheete loose about her, her face uncovered and a white rod in her hand of an ell longe where she shall stand until you begin service at which time your parish clarke shall lead the said penitent by the hand and place her in the middle alley of the church or against the pulpit where she shall stand until the second lesson be ended at the end whereof she shall in penitent manner make this confession following: Vizt.

I doe before almighty god and you his church and congregation here present acknowledge and confess that I have most grievously offended his heavenly Majestie in committing the wicked and detestable offence of fornicacion with Christopher Harbyn for which offence I am hartily sorry and doe unfaynedly repent me of the same. And doe desire you here present not only to pray to god for the forgiveness of my offence but that it may be an example to you all to avoyd the like and I faythfully promise by gods assistance never to offend in the like againe.

The following note is appended to the document:

'Ursula Greene of the parish of Charminster did performe the 19th daye of June 1631 all those things that are enjoyned her to performe by the right of Dr Mason Dean of Sarum'. It is signed by Richard Dike, curate of Charminster.

The men involved in these cases appear to have got off more lightly and were obliged only to pay a fine, or in some case could commute their penance by a fine. Men did not always escape public penance however, and from the numerous examples that survive in the records of the church courts we can quote the case of William Robson of Humshaugh, Northumberland in 1635. He was charged before the church court with having committed adultery with two women and was sentenced to perform public penance 'once in Hexham church, another tyme in Symondburne Church, and the third tyme at the market crosse at Hexham'. He was also imprisoned in the common gaol 'untill he shall have learned the catechisme'.

Another way in which the church was involved in the life of the parish was through the annual perambulation of the parish bounds. This ancient ceremony was essential for maintaining a certain record of the parish bounds in the days before detailed maps, and it was especially important in areas of downland or forest with few natural boundaries. The procession or perambulation was conducted during Rogation week, and in some large parishes it took two or three days to complete; it was the sole survivor of the multitude of processions in which the pre-Reformation church had engaged, and combined the two functions of maintaining and recording afresh the parish boundaries, and offering prayers for seasonable weather and a successful harvest. The processions were often elaborate affairs, following a traditional ritual of meals, drinkings and horseplay, all designed to impress the route upon the memory of the participants and especially upon the children. Churchwardens' accounts frequently contain many references to expenses incurred in the perambulation. For example at St Martin's, Leicester in 1639 'for bread and beere at the Perambulacion 3s 6d. For poynts and ribbon given to the children 3s 0d.' At Deptford, Kent in 1684 the very large sum of £9 1s 0d was spent by the churchwardens on the perambulation, as follows:

Paid Mr Douse for a processioning dinner	£4 7s 0d
Paid Mr Cox at the halfway house for meat, bread, beer, and cakes at the processioning	£2 16s 0d
Paid to the widow Spett for cakes	£1 0s 0d

Paid Rob. Phipps for bread and beer at ye Black-
Jack and Shovel   4s 6d
Paid for 2 bottles of Canary which we had in
Peckham Lane   4s 0d
Paid to make ye boys drink when we came home   1s 0d
Paid more ye same day with ye gentlemen of ye
parish at Mr Douse's after dinner   8s 6d

Even regular processions, however, did not always avoid disputes between neighbouring parishes over their respective boundaries, particularly in areas without any natural features which could be used for demarcation. For example, two neighbouring parishes on the chalk downlands of Dorset, Stratton and Charminster, engaged in a long and expensive dispute over their mutual boundary during the early seventeenth century and the case eventually reached the Exchequer Court in 1616. All the witnesses agreed that the practice of beating the bounds had been carried out each year, but the difficulty had arisen because each party had followed a different route. The Stratton witnesses alleged that

the inhabitants of Charminster within this eight and thirty yeares have altered theyr course of procession . . . and at the first cominge of the now curatt . . . in his first perambulation in procession dyd forsake their old and wonted way and course . . . and did appoynt the said Curatt to goe farther in upon Stratton by Fifty acres or thereabout than they did before, which is the land in variance. . . .

They also stated that the oldest inhabitants of Charminster 'who were men when the others were boys' and who knew that the Stratton allegations were true, had been prevented by threats from attending and giving evidence. The curate was in the difficult position of having to rely on local knowledge of the bounds along which he had to lead the rogationtide procession, particularly in his first years; and the whole dispute illustrates the importance of the topic and the strength of feeling aroused by it.

Gradually the practice died out in most places, partly because enclosures and accurate maps made it superfluous, partly because ratepayers were increasingly reluctant to meet the heavy expenses in food and drink, since those who attended seem to have been intent on eating and drinking as much as possible during the course of the perambulation.

A central figure in the life of the parish was, of course, the parson. It is obviously impossible to generalise about the infinite variety of standards, learning and conduct found among the parish clergy during the seventeenth century and, as always, there is great danger of highlighting those who appear in the surviving records because of some crime, folly or eccentricity, and of forgetting the multitude of clergy who have gone unrecorded because they ministered quietly and faithfully in their parishes and did not attract attention. Most of the parish clergy were little different in wealth, education or life-style from the yeomen and husbandmen among whom they lived. In many parishes the bulk of the tithes went to the impropriator or lay rector whose forbears had acquired them at the dissolution of the monasteries, and many of the clergy were therefore largely dependent upon the income from this glebe. Like their neighbours their wealth was in farm stock, crops and farming equipment. The wills of more than half the clergy in Oxfordshire during the reign of Elizabeth contain evidence of their involvement in farming and this remained the case throughout the seventeenth century. Typical of many of the clergy of the period was Ralph Josselin who was vicar of Earls Colne, Essex, from 1641 to 1683. His average income was about £160 a year, similar to that of a reasonably prosperous yeoman farmer. It was made up of about £60 from his share of the tithes of the parish, together with fees for marriages, funerals and other church dues, the rest of his income deriving from his farming activities supplemented by school-teaching which he did for a few years. The dual concern revealed for example in Josselin's diary entry for Sunday 3 April 1670 was typical of many of his clerical brethren. 'Cow calved; administered the sacrament, only 14 present'. The incumbents' farming concerns also occasionally impinged on the church and churchyard. The vicar of Langtoft in the Yorkshire wolds was excommunicated in 1571 for penning his sheep in the chancel of the church; and at Orford in Norfolk the vicar was reported in 1597 because 'the Churchyard is not decently kept by reason he keepeth his neate (cattle) there and given them meate there'. The lack of education in some of the clergy and their inadequacies as preachers, at a time when lay educational standards were rising, when sermons assumed ever greater importance in church services, and when during the first decades of the seventeenth century the nation was torn by theological disputes, meant that it was often very difficult for the parson to retain the respect of all his flock. In 1617 Richard Christmas, gent., of Sydling St Nicholas, Dorset, was fined £20 for criticising the clergy and ridiculing their sermons. It was alleged that 'he prophaned Religion by setting a Catt on a post in Sydling saying he would make her preach as good a sermon as some of them; he took a text out of Corinth., pincht ye Catt by ye ear and made her crye saying that was a sermon' and went on to compare the cat's performance favourably with that of the local parson.

The collection of tithes was another fruitful source of dispute between the clergy and their parishioners, for the incumbent had the right to collect tithes, either all or in part, from his parishioners, and the complications involved in assessment and collection inevitably gave rise to contention and strife in the parish. In many parishes also the parson had by ancient custom the responsibility of providing a bull and a boar for the use of the parishioners' cows and pigs.

Perhaps the best way of giving a fair and balanced indication of the variety to be found within the ranks of the Anglican clergy during the first half of the seventeenth century, ranging from saints and scholars to rogues, and from wealthy pluralists to poverty-stricken curates, is to take one county, Dorset, and describe briefly a few of the clergy who ministered there. Some of the clergy in the county possessed substantial wealth and were obviously to be included in the ranks of the gentry. For example Richard Russell, who was lord of the manor of West Stafford and also rector there; in 1640 he rebuilt the parish church and his large memorial now dominates the chancel. Gilbert Ironside possessed large estates at Long Bredy where his father had been the incumbent, and he himself became the incumbent of the two neighbouring parishes of Winterborne Steepleton and Winterbourne Abbas. During the Commonwealth his lands were sequestered and he was badly treated, but they were returned to him at the Restoration and in January 1661 he was created bishop of Bristol. The bishopric was very poorly endowed, a fact that led the contemporary commentator Anthony Wood to write of Ironside that '. . . tho' he was never chaplain to any spiritual or temporal lord, or to any King or prince, or enjoyed any dignity in the church, yet being wealthy, he was looked upon as the fittest person to enter upon that mean bishopric'. Dr Gerard Wood was a pluralist with several benefices in Somerset as well as the living of Child Okeford in Dorset where he had a large estate. He was also archdeacon of Wells, and a very active justice of the peace in Dorset. A few of the clergy were scholars of distinction, notably Thomas Fuller the author of *The Worthies of England*, who was incumbent of Broadwindsor from 1634 to 1641. The poet Thomas Bastard was vicar of Bere Regis from 1592 until his death in 1618; he had been a fellow of New College, Oxford, until his bitter satires caused so much resentment that he was forced to leave and take the poorly paid vicarage of Bere Regis. Throughout his years in Dorset he was plagued by poverty, and finally in 1617 was imprisoned for debt at Dorchester where he died in July 1618. His inventory records a total wealth of only £16 1s 5d which included '133 books in his closet' valued at £7 17s 7d. Perhaps the most notable of all the Dorset clergy during the seventeenth century was John White, rector of Holy Trinity, Dorchester, from 1605 to 1648, whose influence extended far beyond the town. His powerful preaching and great piety led Thomas Fuller to write of him in a memorable phrase '. . . he stains all other men's lives with the clearness of his own'. One of John White's most remarkable achievements was in sending a party of puritan settlers to the New World where they hoped to find a religious liberty denied them in England. In 1630 he was instrumental in sending a group from Dorset to settle in New Dorchester, Massachusetts, and several other parties followed during the next few years.

But such men were far from being typical of the Dorset clergy as a whole, for the surviving inventories of most of them show that there was little to distinguish them from the working farmers among whom they lived. A few possessed books of devotion or theology, but most were no more wealthy than their neighbours and, like them, had most of their wealth in their farming stock, crops or equipment.

There is some evidence of the sort of leadership in their communities which was provided by the clergy. At Piddlehinton the struggle of the tenants against the consolidation and enclosure of the demesne lands of the manor was led by the vicar, Thomas Browne, whose charming brass memorial tablet in the church describes him as 'a man greatly beloved'. At Gillingham the two brothers John and Thomas Jessop provided a powerful leadership for the community, the one as parson the other as physician; both are buried in the chancel of the parish church under two effigies, side by side and hand in hand. During the Civil War many of the clergy provided much needed leadership during the difficult times when their congregations were harrassed by the armies of both sides. Some practised as physicians: for example Bartholomew Wesley of Allington, an ancestor of the Methodist founder, had a considerable reputation as a doctor and was described as 'clerke and Phisicion'; Abraham Forrester, rector of Folke, was described by his churchwarden in 1635 as 'being a great practiser of Phisicke in the opinion of the world'. But most eloquent of all, is the fact that again and again the surviving wills and inventories of parishioners are written and drawn up by the parson, who was evidently conscientious in visitation of the sick.

A few were rogues or misfits in their profession. The incumbent of Upwey frequented the local alehouses and 'many times was so drunk that he had to be carried home and could not read divine service on the sabboth day in the morning as he should'. The vicar of Alton Pancras was said in 1609 to neglect the services in order to go to nearby Cheselborne each Sunday 'to footeball upon the sabothe daye', while William Locke, the rector of Askerswell, dabbled in astrology and copied the horoscopes of his two children into the parish register. But such men were exceptional, and for the most part the clergy in Dorset as elsewhere lived quietly in their parishes and ministered to their people without incurring any comment at all, either good or bad.

Until the triumph of the Puritans in the Civil War, parish churches and churchyards continued, as during the pre-Reformation centuries, to be used for all sorts of purposes, many of them secular. People living in remote parts of rural parishes could generally only meet with their neighbours and friends at church on Sundays, and naturally stayed to talk after the service was ended. The incumbent at Rossendale, Lancashire, described in 1603 how 'the congregation of people, men and women, which do daily assemble and come to the church of Rossendale, do use after evening prayers on Sundays and holy days is ended to stay in the church conferring or talking one with another by the space of an hour at the least, except it be in the cold of winter.' Ralph Josselin, who was later Vicar of Earls Colne in Essex, described how as a young man at Steeple Bumpstead during the 1630s he used to walk off alone after services in order to meditate upon the sermon, and did not stay with the rest of the congregation talking in the churchyard. Meetings of the village community also took place in the church. For example at Clayworth in Nottinghamshire, as in many other parishes, the parish met in the church on every Easter Monday to discuss parochial affairs and choose the churchwardens, overseers of the poor, parish constables and other officials. Many parishes of course had a Church House in which such meetings could be held, but there were numerous others where the church was the only building big enough to accommodate a large gathering. The manorial court of Lord Mounteagle at Hornby, Lancashire, was held in the parish church during the seventeenth century; and at Gillingham, Dorset, a meeting of the whole parish in 1624 to discuss the proposals to enclose the royal forest there, was held in the parish church after notice of the meeting had been given from the pulpit on the three previous Sundays. Robert Herrick's well-known lines in praise of the annual round of feasts and revels reminds us of the continuing link between church festivals and secular holidays. Herrick was vicar of the Devonshire parish of Dean Prior on the borders of Dartmoor from 1629 to 1647 and again from 1661 until his death at the age of 83 in

1674. His picture of wakes, ales, dances and revels must have been typical of countless remote country parishes throughout England during the seventeenth century:

> For Sports, for Pagentrie, and Playes,
> Thou hast thy Eves, and Holydayes. . . .
> Thy Wakes, thy Quintels, here thou hast,
> Thy May-poles too with Garlands grac't:
> Thy Morris-dance; thy Whitsun-ale;
> Thy Sheering-feast, which never faile,
> Thy Harvest home; thy Wassaile bowle,
> That's tost up after Fox i'th' Hole;
> Thy Mummeries: thy Twelfe-tide Kings
> And Queenes: thy Christmas revellings.

Manorial and other documents were often left in the parish chest for safe-keeping. Here the church performed an important function, for in view of the frequency of fires in many towns and villages, especially those in areas of England where houses were close together and roofed with thatch, and since there was no other safe place for storage, the church was an obvious repository for important documents. The manorial court rolls of Alrewas, Staffordshire, beginning in 1259, were kept in the parish church, and at Fordington, Dorset, the manorial court records of the Duchy of Cornwall manor were kept in the tower of the parish church, while at Bridport in the same county during the early seventeenth century the parish chest contained documents belonging to several local families who had lodged them there for safe-keeping. Parish churches were also used as repositories for parochial armour and weapons, and for fire-fighting equipment, as well as housing the parish bier. In 1628 there were 190 buckets for fire-fighting in the four churches of Northampton, and at St Botolph, Aldersgate in London, in 1632 there was 'one Brasse Squirt' for the same purpose. Fire-fighting equipment can still be seen in the Dorset churches of Puddletown and Bere Regis, and at Raunds and several other churches in Northamptonshire. Any business of an especially important kind was frequently conducted in the church or churchyard, no doubt in the belief that the hallowed surroundings lent even greater solemnity to agreements arrived at there. Typical of many such agreements was one made between two families at Crowcombe, Somerset, by which £200 was to be paid as a marriage settlement 'upon the font stone of the church of Crowcombe'; and in 1634 John Ekins of Isham, Northamptonshire, paid £100 for houses and land 'upon the communion table in the parish church'.

Justices of the Peace often specified that debts and other payments should be made in the parish church or the church porch. At Brewham, Somerset, Thomas Fryday was convicted in 1627 of being the father of an illegitimate child and ordered 'to pay weekly every sabboth day immediately after eveninge prayer in the Church porch of Bruham aforesaid unto the overseers of the poor 9d.'

PURITAN INFLUENCE

The puritan faction within the church objected to many of the secular uses of churches and churchyards, and their attempts to suppress them during the early seventeenth century provide considerable evidence of contemporary practices. In 1629 Archbishop Harsnet of York ordered that in the parishes within his jurisdiction people should cease to 'walk up and down and talk before and after Divine service, and keep ales and drinkings within the Church, and write their rates on the Communion table'. In 1635 the churchwardens of North Collingham, Nottinghamshire, were ordered to stop manorial courts from meeting within the church and to cease from 'sufferinge laye juries to be in the church and to make their orders at the Communion Table and themselves to be of the Jury'. Churches were also occasionally used as schoolrooms. An episcopal visitation of the diocese of Carlisle in 1702 revealed that schools were being kept in 21 out of the 101 churches examined, and at Westward near Wigton the bishop noted that boys were taught by the curate in the chancel of the parish church, and he was glad to see so many pupils, 'tho' I could have wished them elsewhere', and that they had damaged a monument in the church 'with writing their copies upon it'. At South Leverstone, Nottinghamshire, in 1638 it was reported to the Archdeacon that 'There is a schoole kepte in ye chancell and children whipped there'. Seven high desks had recently been erected, presumably for the children. At Sturton in the same county in 1638 the Archdeacon was told that 'The North Yle of the Westerne (part) of the church is separated and divided from the church by a wall of bordes and converted to a scholehouse where one Marshall teacheth schole'. The churchwardens of Minchinhampton, Gloucestershire, in 1651 evidently had a school in the church, for their accounts record that they 'Payd for stones and makinge a Chimnie in the Chansell for the shoole 6s 3d.' At Long Melford (Suffolk) the Lady Chapel was being used in 1670 as a 'Publick Schoole for Melford' and a multiplication table used by the children survives on the east wall, while in the large church at Boston (Lincolnshire) a school was held in one of the former gild chapels.

The former schoolroom in a gallery survives in the church at Old Dilton, Wiltshire, while at North Cadbury, Somerset, two alphabets can still be seen painted on a wall of the church, a reminder of its former use as a schoolroom. At Winford (Avon) in 1625, during a case before the diocesan court over seating arrangements in the church, elderly inhabitants testified that within their memory there had been no seats in one aisle of the church but that seats had been installed in order that a school might be kept in the church.

The youth of the parish did usuallie stand theare [i.e. in the aisle] to heare divine prayers and the old men of the parishe did theare use to walke upp and downe and talke together before and after prayers.

... theare was a schoolmaster who kepte schoole in the Church of Winford, and because the schollers should have fitt places to sitt in to learne theire lessons the formes and seates were erected and builte upp as well for theire use on the working daies as also for a convenient place for the schollers and other youth of the parish to sitt on on the sabboath and holie days to heare divine service, who before that stoode some in one place and some in another in divers places of the church.

John Evelyn, the diarist, records that he was born at Wotton in the parish of Blackheath (Surrey) in 1620, and that

I was initiated into any rudiments (of education) until near four years of age, and then one Frier taught us at the church porch at Wotton.

Shakespearean audiences were evidently familiar with the practice of having schools in country churches and could recognise immediately the description of 'a pedant that keeps a school i' the church' in *Twelfth Night*. The practice continued in many country parishes during the eighteenth century and for example, Robert Walker, the greatly loved incumbent of Seathwaite (Lancashire) for 67 years, kept a school in his church throughout his ministry; Walker died at the age of 93 in 1802. He was described by Wordsworth in *The Excursion*

> And in his humble dwelling, he appears
> A labourer, with moral virtue girt,
> With spiritual graces, like a glory crowned.

The puritans also endeavoured to suppress the seasonal sports and pastimes, such as festivities at Christmas, Shrove Tuesday, Plough Monday, Whitsun, Midsummer and other traditional holidays which were associated with the parish church, as well as doing their utmost to stop Sunday sports which often took place in the churchyards. The generally successful campaign during the early seventeenth century to discourage these activities, particularly by bringing the participants before the church courts, incidently provides evidence that would otherwise not exist of how widespread and popular such traditional customs and games were. For example, the Archdeacon's visitation of Nottinghamshire in 1638 reveals that ploughs were stored in many of the churches, no doubt for use in the procession round the parish on Plough Monday.

The records of the church courts provide many examples of such occurrences. At Blackthorne, Oxfordshire, in 1584 the churchwardens had to defend themselves against an accusation of allowing the services to be disrupted by merrymaking, and stated that 'on Tewsdaye in ye Whitson weeke at service tyme theyre came a stranger into ye churche with a paynted clothe on his back'; he had apparently come from a neighbouring village to take part in their Whitsun festivities. At Woburn, Bedfordshire, in 1612 the curate baited a bear in the church, and there were regular cock-fights on Shrove Tuesday in the parish church at Knottingley, Yorkshire. The May-day and midsummer 'lords of misrule' in many parts of the country took the form of Robin Hood and Little John, and for example at Yeovil, Somerset, their capers provided one of the main money-raising activities for the parish. At Weymouth and 'in divers Towns and villages within the county of Dorset', the spring and summer festivities of Robin Hood or 'Robarte Hood and Lyttell John' were a regular feature of the early seventeenth century as they had been for many years. They were described as being 'used in the Springe tyme of the yere only of purpose to make sporte and pastyme amonge themselves on Sondaies and other holy daies as also to continewe honest company and mutual society with neighbours'. Such merry-making was essentially connected with the parish church, since it was here that the whole community met together and it was only on Sundays or holy days that they had the leisure to indulge in such frolics, and when people from neighbouring parishes could attend. Like the church ales of which they often formed part, these revels also provided a welcome source of revenue for the churchwardens and the parish. Inevitably there were occasions when the Sunday services were disrupted by the revellers. Francis Milnes of Northallerton, Yorkshire, was brought before the church courts in 1612 'for that he with divers others unknown did, on Easter day last, in the time of afternoon Service, play in the Churchyard there, at a game called Trippett, and did molest and disturbe the Minister there, reading Divine Service with the parishioners there'. The offence was evidently regarded very seriously, for the unfortunate man was sentenced to be whipped. The activities of 'lords and ladies of misrule' in their churches and church-yards got several Oxfordshire churchwardens into trouble with the church courts during the late sixteenth and early seventeenth centuries. At Duns Tew they were accused of allowing 'enterludes and playes in the churche and brawlinge in the churche abowte the same . . . . upon thire wake daye', and before the court they had to confess that certain strangers from neighbouring villages who had come to the wake 'did shoot arrows in the churchyard' during service time; while at Wootton the churchwardens were called to account because of the 'evell rule done in the churche by the lorde and ladie on Midsomer Day' and they were obliged to admit that the young people were 'sumwhat merrie together in the crowning of lordes'. Also in Oxfordshire there was dancing and bowling in the church-yards of Bourton, South Stoke and Goring. At North Cadbury, Somerset, a group of people from nearby Galhampton assembled in 1634 'in time of morning prayer and sermon . . . with a Morrice Daunce and with fiddlers and with a drume and held on theire sporte so neere unto the church' that it was impossible for the parson to conduct the service.

Occasionally churchyards were subjected to other kinds of nuisance. There are frequent reports throughout the seventeenth century of incum-bents allowing their sheep, cattle and pigs to roam in the churchyard, and to traders setting up their stalls there. More serious were the sort of complaints that were made at St James', Bristol, in 1611, where Juliana, wife of Thomas Sanders of Westbury, was accused 'for that she is vehement-lie suspected for being a witche and . . . that she nowe dwelleth in the churche porche'. At the same place in 1674 persons living in the houses which surrounded the churchyard were reported for 'throwing filth from their houses into the churchyard and on the church path to the great annoyance of persons coming to church'. Matthew Walters, a grocer of St Michael's, Bristol was said in 1680 to have a house 'adjoyning to the Churchyard of St Michaels which he useth as a wash house and hath made a hole through the Wall of the said Churchyard through which hee convaieth his water running over the said Churchyard to the great annoiance of the same'.

The widespread popularity and use of games, dancing, maypoles and shooting in churchyards during the early seventeenth century is attested both by the evidence of the church courts and by the account books of the churchwardens who were obliged to pay for the damage done by the players. In the west country the game of fives was very popular, and was played in churchyards against the wall of the church. For example at Martock, Somerset, the evidence of the former fives court is still apparent in the wall of the church, and at Williton in the same county in 1633 two men were bound over by the justices for playing fives in the churchyard:

'there hath been of late an idle game used by tossinge of a ball against the Chapple walle of Williton in a narrow place there betwixt two glasse windows whereby the same windowes were often much torren and defaced to the greate dislike of the inhabitants, especially of those whose seats were next adjoyninge by reason of the drifte in foul weathers, and also of the often greate charges in amendinge the same'.

At Fordington, Dorset, eight people were reported by the churchwardens in 1631 'for that they have played at a game with a Ball called Fives in the churchyard and thereby have broken the glasse of one of the windowes of the church the reparacion whereof is unto the value of 5s od.' At Moulsloe, Buckinghamshire, in 1613 the church windows were broken by children 'that play at catt and stoole ball in the churchyard Sundaies and holidays usualy'. There are countless similar examples of damage caused by such churchyard games, a fact which gave puritan-minded clergy and churchwardens yet another excuse for their suppression.

While we may regret the passing of these colourful activities, there was some force in the Puritan objections to them. It is a mistake to equate the rural pastimes of the seventeenth century with the decorous recreation of a twentieth-century church garden fête. A good deal of licence and drunkenness undoubtedly accompanied festivities such as May Day revels, midsummer frolics and feast-day wakes, and there are too many references to disorders accompanying church ales, to bastards conceived after the festivities and to what the Devon magistrates in 1600 coyly referred to as 'many inconveniences which with modesty cannot be expressed', to be totally ignored. At the same time it is not necessary to go as far as the puritan William Prynne, who wrote that the main purpose of church ales was to enable the common people 'to dance, play, revel, drink and profane God's Sabbaths'. Both James I and Charles I supported the traditional view that sports and pastimes should be allowed and even encouraged on Sunday afternoons. After the Lancashire magistrates in 1617 had attempted to suppress Sunday sports, James I ordered that every minister throughout the country should read a declaration from the pulpit in favour of certain lawful sports to be used on Sundays after divine service. This declaration, sometimes known as the *Book of Sports*, was reissued by Charles I in 1633 after a renewed puritan attempt, this time in Somerset, to prohibit Sunday games. The reading of this declaration gave great cause for disquiet to many Puritan clergy, for example to the curate of Beaminster, Dorset, who according to the churchwardens read the declaration in 1633 very unwillingly:

Mr Spratt our curate was enjoyned to reade the King's Majesty's book touching the lawful recreations of the people upon Sundays after evening prayer, which book hee read accordingly; but having read it, spake of it in the manner; Neighbours (said hee) there is noe one commanded to use these recreations as in this booke is here specifyed, but these lawes are left to everyone's descretion whether you will use them or not use them, therefore I doe advise you rather to obey god's lawes rather than the lawes of the King, or words to that purpose.

THE CIVIL WAR AND THE INTERREGNUM

On the question of church ales and Sunday sports the monarchy and the Anglican establishment won a temporary victory over the puritan faction during the 1630s, and especially while the church was ruled by Archbishop Laud. But the turn of the puritans was to come, for with the success of the Parliamentary cause in the Civil War the puritan religious and political ideas triumphed. During the course of the Civil War, as troops moved all over the country there was a great deal of destruction and damage to churches and church property. Many of the Parliamentarians saw the church and the monarchy as joint enemies, and were eager to purge the parish churches of what they considered the surviving relics of popery, so that works of art and things of great beauty which had escaped destruction during the sixteenth century fell victim to puritan zeal during the 1640s. Stained glass was smashed, statues were defaced or destroyed, vestments cut up or torn to bits and organs, service-books and carved woodwork burnt. Much of the desecration of churches which is conventionally ascribed to Oliver Cromwell in popular tradition was in fact caused by troops, generally parliamentarian but occasionally also royalist, out of the control of their officers.

Most of the Anglican clergy had supported or at least sympathised with the royalist party, and with the defeat of the King in 1646 many of the clergy, perhaps a third of the whole number, were ejected from their benefices as 'delinquents' or 'malignants' and replaced by puritan ministers. The sufferings endured by some of the clergy were extremely harsh. The royalist incumbent at Pontefract was hanged by the Parliamentary army, the aged vicar of Tarrington was shot through the head when he told a troop of Parliamentarians that he supported 'God and the King';

many others suffered ill-treatment and pillage of their possessions as well as loss of their benefices, like Humphrey Betty of Little Petherick, Cornwall, who was driven out of his parish 'all naked'. The use of the Book of Common Prayer was strictly forbidden, and in its place a *Directory* for public worship was issued, which left considerable latitude for individual ministers in the conduct of the services. The impact of the changes in the services in parish churches therefore varied from place to place. But as well as new services most congregations also witnessed other changes, for the triumph of the puritans unleashed another holocaust of destruction. Screens, stalls, crosses, statues, organs, stained glass, paintings and vestments which had escaped earlier attacks were now broken or defaced. The royal arms were removed, and communion tables—which under Archbishop Laud's regime during the 1630s had been carefully enclosed with rails, 'altarwise', at the east end of the chancel—were brought out into the body of the church, where the congregation could gather around them; often seats were provided around the table to make the Holy Communion as much of a commemorative service and as little like the sacrament of the Mass as possible. The pulpit and the sermon became the central focus of the church; and fonts were frequently torn out or defaced since they were associated with popish rites. The parish register of Keeston, Kent, contains the entry for 23 April 1643, 'Our church was defaced, our font thrown downe and new formes of prayer appointed'. Likewise Ralph Josselin, the puritan vicar of Earls Colne, Essex, recorded with satisfaction in his diary for Michaelmas 1641 that he had been able to strip his church of the surviving medieval statues, stained glass and wall-paintings, 'upon an order of House of Commons to that purpose wee tooke downe all (images) and pictures and such like glasses'. Men like Josselin of course welcomed the changes, and rejoiced greatly when Parliament removed 'the heavy burthen of the booke of Common prayer'.

The most notorious inconoclast of this period was William Dowsing, who during 1643 and 1644 visited several score of churches in Cambridgeshire and Suffolk, breaking and destroying everything that could be held to be superstitious or papist—images, glass, pictures, crosses, and even carvings and brasses on tombs. Dowsing is however only the most infamous of a large number of similar fanatics who ranged through the country inflicting untold damage upon parish churches.

In the contemporary atmosphere of destruction and iconoclasm few parish churches escaped and there were few additions either to furnishings or buildings. An exception was the church at Staunton Harold in Leicester-shire which was built by the royalist Shirley family during the Common-wealth as a gesture of defiance to the Parliamentary government. The tower bears the following inscription:

> In the yeare 1653
> When all thinges sacred were throughout ye nation
> Either demollisht or profaned
> Sir Robert Shirley, Barronet
> Founded this church
> Whose singular praise it is
> to have done the best thinges in ye worst times
> And
> hoped them in the most callamitous
> The righteous shall be had in everlasting remembrance.

With the return of the king in 1660 came the return of the Anglican church. The 'intruded' ministers were removed and in many parishes those they had replaced resumed their offices and their rights to tithes and other dues. The use of the Book of Common Prayer was revived, and the book was reissued with a few minor changes in 1662. The interior arrangement of parish churches was restored, with the altar at the east end of the chancel, decently railed. The essential link between the monarchy and the church was emphasised by the erection of the royal coat of arms in parish churches throughout the country, and appropriate texts also appeared on the walls, drawing attention to the christian duty of obedience to established authority and to the wickedness of rebellion; these included 'The powers that be are ordained of God' and 'My son, fear God and the King, and meddle not with them that are given to change'. A few of these survive and can still be found in parish churches. But the upheavals and changes of the previous 20 years had been too profound to admit of total restoration. Nonconformity had now to be recognised in almost every parish as an established fact of religious life, and no longer could the Anglican church claim to include all Christians within each parish. It is from the Restoration of 1660 that the real beginning of the deep and significant division of English social life between 'church' and 'chapel' can be dated. The gulf thus created was to remain until the twentieth century, a division that touched all aspects of life and affected attitudes to society, to politics, to education and to economic life, and which had an immeasureable impact upon the development of the nation.

The role of the parish church and its officials in village life during the

18. *Interior of Beckington Church, Somerset, by W. W. Wheatley, c 1846*
A typical unrestored parish church interior.

19. *Restoration in Progress, Broadwindsor, Dorset, 1867–8* An early photograph showing the extent to which many Victorian 'restorations' went, involving virtually the complete reconstruction of the church.

20. *Friendly Society Banner, Stogursey, Somerset* One of several heavy wooden 'banners' which are still kept in the parish church. Others show figures and emblems such as 'Britannia', 'Ceres' and 'Success to Trade'.

seventeenth and eighteenth centuries can be reconstructed in detail from the evidence of the many hundreds of surviving churchwardens' accounts. The churchwardens played a part in the parish in many ways more important than the parson. From the sixteenth century onwards they had heaped upon them a mass of secular duties relating to matters as diverse as the care of the poor, the maintenance of the highways and the control of vermin, all of them having little relevance to their main and original function of maintaining the church and providing the things necessary for the conduct of the services. An indication of the variety of their concerns is seen in the churchwardens' accounts for Cerne Abbas (Dorset) in 1686. They paid for repairs and maintenance of the church, for a new Book of Common Prayer, for bread and wine for the sacrament and for the washing of the surplice and altar cloth; in addition they paid the ringers for ringing the bells on the King's birthday, on 5 November and on 29 May—the latter being the day on which the King's restoration was celebrated. They contributed money to repatriate various English sailors who had been captured by Turkish pirates in the Mediterranean; for the relief of 'Mary Francis and Benjamin Cimber and their children begging who had lost all their goods by fire'; they relieved 14 men who claimed to have been shipwrecked on the Dorset coast; they sent money to help the French Protestants who were being persecuted for their religion; they paid for the repair of the church clock and for repairs to the local roads. And throughout the year they rewarded those who brought birds and animals regarded as vermin; the total of vermin for the year was

85 dozen sparrows heads (the term 'sparrow' presumably covered all small birds)
37 hedgehogs
 9 polecats
 9 stoats
 4 foxes

During the eighteenth century the churchwardens also had responsibility for the fire-engine and for keeping its leather pipes oiled and supple. There are constant references to expenditure on 'the engine'; typical is the entry for 1753

For oyling the pipes of the Engion	1s 6d
For oyl and Cleaning of ye Engion	1s 6d

The victories of the British armies during the wars of the eighteenth century also involved the churchwardens in expenditure on the ringers who were paid to celebrate the triumphs. For example, in the great 'year of victories' 1759 the Cerne Abbas accounts include the entries

Gave the Ringers when Prince Ferdinand Defeated the French in jarmony	6s od
Gave the Ringers when Quebeck was taken	5s od

From the numerous surviving churchwardens' accounts we also get a view of the services in parish churches, the singers and musicians, the parish clerk, the bell-ringers and other essential dignitaries of the church which will be discussed in the next chapter.

6. Sermons and sober decency

During the eighteenth century the Anglican church settled down to a quiet routine of services and sermons, secure in its position as an essential part of the established order and untroubled by the sort of controversies which had marked the previous century. It is true that there were excitements such as the Jacobite rebellions and various theological disputes, and in the later eighteenth and early nineteenth centuries the church was torn by the rise and eventual separation of the Methodists, but nonetheless in most parishes the prevailing atmosphere of the period was of a calm, staid acceptance of the *status quo* and a distrust of anything which smacked of 'enthusiasm' or fervour. The church remained subservient to the civil government; the bishops were selected on political grounds or for their birth and connections, and were expected to spend a major part of their time in parliament where their votes in the house of Lords were of great importance to successive governments. In addition, many dioceses remained enormous in extent, like that of Lincoln which stretched over five counties from the Humber to the Thames, and contained 1,312 parishes; or the diocese of Exeter which included the whole of Devon and Cornwall. In such vast areas, adequate and efficient episcopal control was inevitably lacking. The use of suffragan or assistant bishops had ceased after the Reformation, and there was no provision for an elderly or infirm bishop to retire. It was an impossible task for a single bishop, however energetic, adequately to supervise the clergy and confirm the laity in such huge dioceses, particularly in view of the difficulties of travel and the other calls upon their time. Confirmation tours or visitations could generally only be conducted during the summer months, and to arrange such a tour over a large diocese meant careful planning and a consideration of the roads, the weather, the state of the harvest, market-days and accommodation. Moreover since bishoprics varied greatly in their endowments, the modestly paid were regarded as no more than stepping stones to more lucrative sees, and few bishops remained for long in the worst-paid dioceses. For example, the income of the bishopric of Bristol was among the lowest, so that its bishops devoted much of their time to ensuring that they were rapidly translated to a richer see, and during the eighteenth century few bishops remained at Bristol for more than three years. The same was true of several other bishoprics.

Among the clergy there was a great gulf between the richer, beneficed clergy, many of them holding more than one living, and the poorly paid curates who did most of the work. During the eighteenth century the income and status of the more fortunate clergy increased substantially as rising land-values, improved agricultural production and higher prices for farm produce raised the value of their tithes. The opulent life-style of the clergy in the well-endowed parishes is still evident from the fine Georgian parsonage houses which survive in so many places, and also from the expensive and ornate monuments with which they burdened the chancels of their parish churches. But in many English parishes any increase in the value of the tithes went into the pockets of the lay rectors or 'impropriators', and the vicar or curate saw little benefit from it. There was a large army of un-beneficed curates employed by the richer, pluralist clergy, and few of these unfortunates, without either benefice or security, were paid more than £40 per annum. The inadequacy of the stipends of the lower-paid clergy was recognised throughout the period, and as early as 1704 Queen Anne's Bounty was established whereby the Queen set up a fund to supplement the incomes of the poorer clergy, but poverty and distress continued among them throughout the period. Smollett's curate in his novel *Roderick Random* published in 1748, expressed the feelings of many of the lower-paid clergy towards the rich pluralists whose work they did; after meeting his vicar at an inn, he cried,

There the old rascal goes, and the d—l go with him. You see how the world wags, gentlemen. By Gad, this rogue of a vicar does not deserve to live; and yet he has two livings worth £400 *per annum*, while poor I am fain to do all his drudgery, and ride twenty miles every Sunday to preach; for what? why truly, for £20 a year.

The practice of one man holding several benefices was constantly decried by critics of the Church, but little was done to alter the situation until the nineteenth century. Pluralism sprang both from the practice of well-connected and influential clergy acquiring several benefices merely as a source of income, appointing lowly-paid curates to do the work of the parish, and also from the fact that the incomes of some parishes were insufficient to support a resident clergyman. It has to be remembered that there was no provision for ill-health or old age among the clergy, and in some places the population was so small as not to warrant a resident incumbent. Moreover many parishes had no suitable house for the clergy, although the disrepair or inadequacy of many parsonage houses was itself often the direct result of long years without a resident incumbent.

In York diocese in 1743, out of the 836 parishes in the diocese 393 had non-resident incumbents, while in Devon in 1779, 159 out of the 390 incumbents were non-resident; many of the parishes were served by curates, but frequently the curates themselves undertook the care of more than one parish. Similarly a survey of Wiltshire in 1783 showed that of the 262 parishes, 124 had non-resident incumbents. Hannah More, who did so much to relieve poverty and lack of education among the people of north Somerset, reported in 1796 that 'we have in this neighbourhood thirteen adjoining parishes without so much as a resident curate'; she also commented on the children of the area that 'hardly any had ever seen the inside of a church since they were christened'.

An episcopal visitation of the diocese of Bristol in 1735 revealed both the reasons for much of the non-residence and its consequences. The diocese at that time included the county of Dorset, and the bishop found that the rector of Chilfrome 'has not resided since his institution and lives at Westbourn in Sussex. Mr Osborn, vicar of Bradpole is his curate'. The rector of Langton Herring was a fellow of Kings College, Cambridge, but actually resided at Eton where he was tutor to Lord Milton's sons. The incumbent of Wyke Regis also lived at Eton 'on account of his wife's ill-health and for the education of his boys'. At Weston Buckhorn the Bishop noted wryly that the rector 'does not reside and complains much of ill-health, tho' he looks the picture of health itself'. The consequences of this widespread non-residence and pluralism were that few parishes had more than one service on a Sunday and many were without a resident minister. At most places the Holy Communion was celebrated only three times a year and the number of communicants was pitifully small, while in most of the towns and larger villages there were large congregations of dissenters—Baptists, Congregationalists, Quakers and a few Catholics. The visitation of 1735 also revealed that Lyme Regis, with its strong Puritan tradition and history of resistance to the royal forces during the Civil War, was still strongly independent, and the bishop noted that 'Incumbent Mr Syms, good, his predecessor Mr Hallett had been minister there sixty years, seldom used the surplice or conformed in any respect strictly to the rules of the church. This did not lessen the number of Dissenters and now ten out of sixteen and the generality of the town are such'. The bishop also observed that in the parish church at Lyme Regis the communion table was still placed in the middle of the chancel as had been the practice during the Commonwealth, 'the Communion table not set altarwise but with a rail quite round it in the middle of the Chancell'.

For the well-paid beneficed clergy or the pluralists, the Church during the eighteenth century provided a very comfortable living with a minimal number of duties, and it became an attractive career for younger sons or the close relatives of gentry families. As clerical diaries such as that of James Woodforde show, the better-off clergy could live in a style little different from the country squire, were received as equals by the gentry, and could devote their days to country sports, dining, the management of their glebe lands and the collection of their tithes, and they could play a part in local affairs by serving as justices of the peace. The career offered such attractions that, not surprisingly, there are many examples during the period of clerical dynasties where the members of one family successively occupied a benefice or group of neighbouring benefices over long periods. For example, from 1698 to 1887 nine members of the Carwithen family were successive rectors of the Devonshire parish of Manaton on the borders of Dartmoor, where they were patrons of the living and owners of a large estate. In the same county at Roseash, the Southcombe family who owned most of the land in the parish were rectors without intermission from 1675 to 1881. At Minstead and Sopley in Hampshire the Willis-Compton family held the livings from 1759 until 1928.

Once instituted into a benefice, a clergyman was very difficult to dislodge, since only heresy or gross immorality would provide suitable grounds, and he could only be deprived through the cumbersome machinery of the church courts. In view of their security as well as of their isolation in country parishes, it is hardly surprising that many of the clergy became a law unto themselves in their parishes and that there are numerous eighteenth-century examples both of scandalous neglect and of notable eccentrics. One instance concerns the three parishes of St Buryan, St Levan and Sennen in the far west of Cornwall. These parishes were known as 'the Deanery of Buryan' and were a royal peculiar, that is they were exempt from the control of the bishop of the diocese, and were in the gift of the Crown. In 1816 the Hon. Fitzroy Stanhope, who had served with distinction in the army during the Napoleonic War and had lost a leg in fighting at Waterloo, applied to the Duke of York, then Commander-in-Chief, for a pension and was offered instead the Deanery of Buryan. The benefice was worth about £1,000 a year, and there were no duties except the payment of curates to serve the parishes. Stanhope was duly ordained and appointed to the benefice in 1817; he continued to hold it, without ever going there, for a period of 47 years. His curate at St Buryan suffered from an unfortunate psychological disorder, and had to be fastened to the reading desk before he could conduct the service. On weekdays he supplemented his low salary by playing the fiddle at the village inn. At nearby Wendron the vicar, Thomas Wills, was instituted in 1748 and remained as vicar for 53 years. A later vicar of Wendron wrote of him that

Mr Wills belonged to a type of country clergyman only too common before the great church revival of the nineteenth century . . . began to restore a high standard of ministerial life and work. He was a hunting parson and farmed Trenethick, where he kept a pack of hounds. He has left in the parish a most deplorable reputation for scandalous neglect of his ordination vows —the universal tradition (no doubt slightly exaggerated as usual) is that he never entered the church for the 53 years he was vicar. I find his signature in the Marriage Register, but in that Register only, three or four times. . . . A contemporary poem tells how the vicar's cow died and how he was dissuaded from giving the flesh to his hounds as "it might infect the kennel through". Instead he sent a message around the parish announcing that there would be a free distribution of beef to the poor.

Few of the clergy were of course so neglectful of their duties as this. Many were of necessity busy upon their glebe farms, others were occupied with local affairs as justices of the peace or were engaged in their own studies, for the eighteenth-century church produced an impressive array of scholars among its clergy, ranging from Bishops Berkeley and Butler in philosophy to Gilbert White the naturalist, William Stukeley the archaeologist and Jethro Tull the agricultural reformer and inventor. Samuel Carter, the vicar of St Martin's, Leicester, during the early eighteenth century was absorbed by the history and antiquities of his neighbourhood, and his notes form the basis of John Nichols' later history. John Collinson in Somerset and John Hutchins in Dorset were both parish clergymen who wrote monumental histories of their counties, and there were many other eighteenth-century clerics similarly involved in the study of local history, antiquities, natural history and geology. It was of such men that it was somewhat unkindly said 'The country clergy are constant readers of the *Gentlemen's Magazine*, deep in the antiquities of inn signs, speculations as to what becomes of swallows in the winter, and whether hedgehogs or other urchins are most justly accused of sucking milch cows dry at night'. In its clergy, as in so much else about its organisation and attitudes, the eighteenth-century church did no more than mirror the prevailing opinions in the upper classes of contemporary society to which it was so closely tied, and where enormous significance was attached to birth, breeding, connections, wealth and the possession of land. It would be unjust to judge the standards of the eighteenth century from the viewpoint of the twentieth.

Turning to the parish churches themselves, the use which was made of them and the part they played in community life during the eighteenth and early nineteenth centuries, it is clear that in most places the time was now past when the church and churchyard were used for anything other than for the services and for the burial of the dead. No longer did church-wardens' income derive from games, plays and fund-raising activities centred upon church or church-house and churchyard. In the majority of parishes the church was locked during weekdays, and in any case was filled with the large private pews of those wealthy enough to afford the social prestige which they conferred; almost everywhere the church-houses had lost their original function and had either fallen into ruin or had become dwellings, inns, poor-houses, or schools; and in the church-yard the growing practice of erecting headstones, footstones and elaborate tombs over the graves meant that no longer was there suitable open space for public recreation.

There is little evidence that the church buildings were neglected. It is of course possible to find examples from any century of ruinous or dilapi-dated churches, but it was the primary duty of churchwardens to maintain their fabric and the evidence of innumerable churchwardens' accounts from all over the country confirms that they did so. Their income now came, not from church ales and from the pious offerings of the laity, but from rents for church lands, payments for pews and from church rates levied upon householders. The habit of eighteenth-century churchwardens of commemorating any notable piece of building work, repair or restora-tion in their parish church by erecting a large stone or lead slab somewhere on the building, bearing prominently their own names or initials, provides proof in countless churches of the extent and regularity of maintenance. Although there are exceptions, it is not in general true to say that the sweeping Victorian restorations were made necessary by eighteenth-century neglect of the buildings; rather the restorations were carried out because of changed religious ideas and fashions, and also because of the inevitable difficulties inseparable from any attempt to bring medieval buildings up to a standard acceptable to professional Victorian architects. For the interior decoration of their churches eighteenth-century churchwardens depended almost entirely upon whitewash. It was cheap and effective, and made for a light and airy building in which to hear the sermons which formed such an important part of the services. Further decoration was provided at the east end of the chancel by the Ten Commandments, the Creed and the Lord's Prayer, either painted directly on to the walls or upon boards arranged around the altar. Suitable texts could also easily be applied to the whitewashed walls of the nave. Another prominent feature of the interior decoration of the church was the royal coat of arms. Frequently these were the work of a local artist or signwriter, and were more notable for their vigour of execution—with fearsome and aggressively masculine lion and unicorn—than for any artistic merit or even heraldic accuracy. Nonetheless they symbolised the essential link between Church and State, and the role of the established church in the life of the nation.

Sermons were a much more regular feature of the services than was the Holy Communion, and the pulpit occupied a correspondingly more important place in the interior arrangement of the church. In most parish churches the altar was to be found, decently railed, at the east end of the chancel, but several country churches for long preserved the puritan arrangement, introduced during the Commonwealth, whereby the altar was placed centrally in the chancel, often standing 'tablewise' east and west. The altar was covered with a cloth or 'carpet' of silk or other material, upon which was laid a white linen cloth on those few occasions in the year when the Holy Communion was celebrated. If there was any decoration at all, it consisted only of a pair of candlesticks; until the nineteenth century it was rare to find a cross on the altar. The main focus of attention in the eighteenth-century parish church was the pulpit and reading-desk, often also combined with a desk for the parish clerk. Many of these 'three-decker' pulpits, complete with their large sounding-board and elaborate pulpit cushion, survive and provide, perhaps more clearly than anything else, a reminder of the atmosphere and priorities of eighteenth-century Anglicanism. An alternative arrangement which was popular in the later eighteenth century was a twin pulpit and reading desk, each of the same size, and elevated above the pews of the congregation and often placed on either side of the chancel or even half-way down the nave, so that all could hear clearly. This arrangement, which makes the church look as though it has two pulpits, can still be seen for example at Haughton-le-Skerne, County Durham; Wolverton, Hampshire; Mildenall, Wiltshire; and Portland, Dorset. It was also during this period that the splendid brass chandeliers were installed which still form such an attractive feature of many parish churches.

In parishes with a resident squire or gentry family, their private pew occupied a favoured and prominent place, sometimes in the chancel itself. Some of these pews were elaborately furnished with a fireplace, tables, chairs and sofas, and had their own separate entrance. In them the family sat divorced from their tenants in the nave, as though in a private drawing-room, surrounded by the ornate monuments of their ancestors, as if to emphasize still further the advantages of breeding and inherited wealth. Good examples of such pews can still be seen at Breedon-on-the-Hill, Leicestershire, Chaddleworth, Berkshire, Whalley, Lancashire and Hinton St George, Somerset, as well as in many other churches. The age saw no incongruity in apportioning church seats in accordance with social status. The importance attached to rank was one of the outstanding characteristics of the age, though perhaps not everyone would have gone as far as the Duchess of Buckingham, who wrote in 1743 to Selina, Countess of Huntingdon

I thank your ladyship for the information concerning the Methodist preachers. Their doctrines are most repulsive, and strongly tinctured with impertinence, and disrespect towards their superiors. It is monstrous to be told that you have a heart as sinful as the common wretches that crawl the earth. I cannot but wonder that your ladyship should relish any sentiments so much at variance with high rank and good peerage.

The naves were filled with the square box-pews of the wealthier members of the congregation, in which each family sat facing each other, in comparative seclusion. A practical advantage of such pews was that they protected the occupants from draughts, an important consideration in large, unheated churches. Those unable to afford pew-rents were accommodated on forms in the aisles, at the back of the church or in the gallery.

A major reason why the Church of England failed to cope adequately with the changing conditions of the eighteenth century, and in particular failed to provide for the rapidly growing population in many towns and villages, was because of the constraints imposed by the parochial system. The parish was much more than a convenient unit of church administration. It was a complex, legal web of property rights, financial interests, tithe dues and temporal as well as spiritual responsibilities. To change this ancient system was extremely difficult, and before 1818 a private Act of Parliament was required to create a new parish or divide an existing one. Consequently the situation increasingly occurred in populous parishes during the eighteenth century that not all the parishioners who wished to obtain pews in their parish church could do so. Many of the middle classes, who would have scorned to sit with the lower orders in the free seats at the back or in the gallery, were thus effectively excluded from their churches. In 1715 the inhabitants of Whitehaven, Cumberland, petitioned for a new church:

... as the inhabitants of the town of Whitehaven ... being greatly increased since the building of the present church or chapel there cannot now be all decently contained therein, whereby great numbers of the said inhabitants are put under a necessity either of staying at home, neglecting the public worship of Almighty God or of going to other churches in the country at a great distance and with much inconveniency, and several others may be induced for want of other accommodation to resort to the places of worship amongst those that dissent from the Church of England, and whereas the said town of Whitehaven being still in a growing condition some other place for public worship in the town is like to be daily more necessary and the want thereof attended with worse consequences.

At the other end of the country in Truro, Cornwall, in 1806 the editor of the local newspaper *The Royal Cornwall Gazette* wrote to the vicar of St Mary's complaining that he could not obtain seats for himself and his family in the church.

I have been nearly three years resident in this town, and hope to finish my days here. I have a pretty numerous family, eight children (with a probability of more) besides apprentices. It is my wish to bring up this numerous family members of our Church Establishment, and, with this in view I have repeatedly solicited the churchwardens to find me room in the church. I am now again called upon for payment of the Church Rate, without yet being able to get my family accommodated within its walls. ...

If the family of the editor of a staunchly Tory local newspaper cou d not find room in the church, we can imagine the problems of less influential members of the community. In this connection it is impossible to resist quoting a letter addressed to Bishop Henry Phillpotts, the bishop of Exeter, which although written some time later, does show the problems which rented seats and space-consuming box-pews could cause. The letter was written from Honiton, Devon, in 1841:

The Right Honable Filpot, Bishop of Exeter. The poor inhabetence of

Honiton wiches me to in form your Lordshep that the sets wich leads from the stars the length of the Church ech side was sets fexed again the wall and wrote down Free Seets, . . . for the poor to set in as the light of the windos inabled them to read thar books. . . . now the have taken it down wich in consequenc I am sorey two say that for want of them sets the are leving the Church. If your Lordshep shold think proper to have them sets fixed a gain the poor old be very thinkefull.

Gilbert White, the antiquarian and naturalist, who was curate of Selborne in Hampshire from 1751 to 1793, described the haphazard arrangement of private pews within his church,

Nothing can be more irregular than the pews of this church, which are of all dimensions and heights, being patched up according to the fancy of the owners.

The tenacity with which parishioners clung to their right to a private pew can be illustrated from a dispute at Warminster (Wiltshire) which eventually developed into a protracted lawsuit. The complicated story is summarised in the *Victoria County History of Wiltshire, Vol. VIII*, as follows:

From the seventeenth century it had been the custom for the church-wardens to grant space in the church on which pews could be erected, which could then be the subject of lease, conveyance, or bequest by the families which occupied them. This kind of traffic, not unique to War-minster, seems to have reached here an uncommon intensity, perhaps because of the limited church accommodation. In the late eighteenth century the vestry tried to limit the tenure of pews to leasehold for three lives, but in the 1830's four pews were regarded as freehold, belonging to the manor houses of Portway, Smallbrook, and Boreham, and to the house in East Street formerly belonging to the manor of Warminster Scudamore, but held since the seventeenth century by the Halliday family. It was the Halliday pew which caused the trouble. At the restoration of the church Philipps (the Vicar) had it removed; J. E. Halliday, who was a dissenter, began an action against the vicar for the pew to be replaced, which he won in the House of Lords in 1891. The pew was not put back in the church until 1897, when some friends of Halliday wished to attend a service. Halliday was very unpopular in the town, and the pew was soon removed from the church by night, smashed and partially burnt. It was, however, roughly repaired and put back under police escort, fixed to the floor by a blacksmith, and it remained on its site in the south chancel aisle until after its owner's death in 1913, when it was finally surrendered.

The right to private pews could have odd consequences. On the island of Portland it was decided during the mid-eighteenth century to abandon the old church of St Andrews which was inconveniently situated and in a bad state of repair, and instead to build a fine new church in the centre of the island. One of the ways in which money was raised for the new church was to sell the freehold right to sit in particular pews in the church. The new church was duly built and consecrated in 1766. The church, dedicated to St George, is a superb example of the sort of interior arrangement favoured during the eighteenth century, adapted for preaching and with very little emphasis given to the altar. By the end of the nineteenth century, however, such interior layout was no longer fashionable or convenient and it was proposed to take out the large box-pews and reconstruct the interior of the church. But the practice of partiple inheritance or *gavelkind*—whereby a man's property was commonly divided in equal shares amongst his sons, or for want of sons, among his daughters—had survived on the island of Portland: the result was that by the late nineteenth century many hundreds of people possessed part-shares in the pews of St Georges, and it was an impossible task to secure the agreement of such a large number to any change in the church. Incredibly therefore it was decided that the only solution was to abandon St Georges', and to build a completely new church a short distance away. The new church, All Saints', was consecrated in 1917.

The problem of accommodating all who wished to attend was not, however, one that afflicted by any means all parish churches during the eighteenth century, for by the early part of the century the growth of various nonconformist churches had already taken many people away from the Anglican church, and during the century a great many more were to leave, particularly with the remarkable growth of Methodism and the eventual separation of the Methodists from the Church of England. The movement was already apparent to Daniel Defoe, himself a dissenter, when he visited Southwold, Suffolk, in the 1720s and wrote that he was

surprised to see an extraordinarily large church, capable of receiving five or six thousand people, and but twenty-seven in it besides the parson and the clerk; but at the same time the meeting house of the Dissenters was full to the very doors, having as I guessed six to eight hundred people in it.

In those parishes where there was a resident incumbent, the common practice was to have two services each Sunday, matins at 11.00 a.m., generally with a sermon, and evensong at 3.00 p.m. A later evening service would have been impossible during the winter months since most churches lacked adequate lighting and were without heating. The morning service was often very long, including the litany besides a lengthy sermon. Many parishes, however, had only one service each Sunday, often alternate morning and afternoon services. A visitation of the diocese of York in 1743 showed that only 383 parish churches out of 836 had two services each Sunday. The frequency with which the Holy Communion was celebrated varied greatly, depending upon the attitude of the incumbent or curate. By far the most common practice, however, was a celebration of this sacrament four times a year, at Christmas, Easter, Whitsun and Michaelmas. The number of communicants was generally very low and declined during the period. For example, in the diocese of Exeter between 1779 and 1821 the number of communicants decreased by 23 per cent in spite of a large increase in the population. Parson James Woodforde, who was the resident and well-liked incumbent of Weston Longeville, Norfolk from 1776 to 1803, had a population in his parish of about 360 but never had more than 30 at Communion and generally the number was much lower. In contrast as many as 60 children under fourteen came each year to the Vicarage on St Valentine's day, following an ancient custom which Woodforde continued whereby each child who could say 'Good Morrow, Valentine' received a penny. Various reasons were suggested by the clergy for the low number of communicants, ranging from want of decent clothing to the reason put forward by the incumbent of Goring, Oxfordshire in 1738, 'ye motives of Negligence and Want of due Regard and lively Sense of their Duty'. However, he consoled himself with the thought that the absentees 'are Persons of the Lowest Rank'. Archbishop Secker, one of the most notable and conscientious of the eighteenth-century archbishops of Canterbury, complained that 'Some imagine that the Sacrament belongs only to persons of advanced years, or great leisure, or high attainment in religion, and it is a very dangerous thing for common persons to venture on'. The vicar of St Mary Magdalen's, Oxford, in a city which might have been thought to be lavishly endowed with clergy and churches, explained the lack of attendance at church services without difficulty.

It must be confessed yt there are in this Parish (especially among the poorer sort) great numbers of Absentees from ye Publick worship of Almy. God. This Scandalous and lamentable Neglect is (I fear) in most Persons ye Effect of a Worldly, Carnal, unthinking or Irreligious Disposition of Mind, Occasioned by ye want of an Early Instruction in ye Principles of Duties of Christianity.

In view of the small number of communicants, a startling feature of churchwardens' accounts of the seventeenth and eighteenth centuries is the large quantities of wine which were purchased for the Sacrament. For example at Wirksworth, Derbyshire, 31 quarts of wine were bought for the Communion in 1679, and many eighteenth-century churchwardens' accounts provide examples of similar large quantities being purchased.

The reason for such apparently excessive amounts may be that it was the practice for communicants to drink deeply from the chalice, or it may be that the churchwardens kept some for themselves. Perhaps the explanation lies in the rubric of the Book of Common Prayers which orders that 'if any of the Bread and Wine remain unconsecrated, the Curate shall have it to his own use'. Various kinds of wine are mentioned as being purchased for the Communion, among them Malmsey, Muscadel, Sack, Canary and Claret. In a few churches it was the practice to hold separate Communion services, one for the upper and middle classes, the other for the lower orders. At the former more expensive wine was provided, while the poor members of the congregation were given the cheaper claret. The responsibility for providing the bread and wine for the Sacrament rested upon the churchwardens. In 1738 the vicar of Bladen near Woodstock, Oxfordshire, complained to the bishop of 'an Abuse not peculiar to this place, but frequent in Many; viz. by ye Negligence of Church-Wardens and Profanity of Bakers and Vintners, ye Worst of Bread and Wine is often provided for ye H. Sacrament. Nothing being more Common that to have ye former ye most Stale or Coarse, or Musty; and ye latter, ye most Sour, or Vapid yt can be got'.

An important part in parish-church services was played by the parish clerk, whose duties included saying the responses and 'Amens', and reading the lessons and leading the congregation in the recitation or singing of the psalms and a hymn, as well as cleaning the church. Not all parish clerks were well educated or good readers and singers, and many are the stories of their mistakes and mispronunciations. Many parish clerks must have resembled the clerk at Mapperton, Dorset, of whom the churchwardens reported 'We have not a sufficient parishe clerke that can read the first lesson: but yet the parishioners are well pleased with him for that he keepeth the church clenlie'. The parish clerk also engaged in numerous other activities in and around the church and churchyard. In the seventeenth century the duties of the parish clerk at North Nibley (Gloucestershire) had been defined as follows:

At a publicke meeting May 18 1639, 20 of the Inhabitants being present it was thus concluded concerning the Parish Clerke That the said Clerke for the time being shall be serviceable to the Minster and shall ring the bells at times convenient and appointed, and also shall be carefull to preserve the Ornaments of the church and keepe the Churche cleane, sweeping the same once every weeke, with all the seates therein. He shall every morning presently after 4 and every night presently after 8 of the Clocke ring the Bell commonly called the Cover-feu Bell betweene the festivall day of St

Michaell and the Annunciation, and shall keepe the Clocke according to his best skill for the whole yeare about.

He shall doe all other dutyes as shall belong unto his place. For his wages it is concluded that every severall householder in the Parrish shall pay 4d by the yeare, viz 2d at the feast of Easter and 2d at the feast of St Michael the Archangel upon the first demand.

That the Churchwardens for the time being shall pay in consideration of ringing the bell as aforesaid 6s 8d at the festival day of St Thomas and 6s 8d at the Annunciation yearly.

For putting upp a banns and attending at the Solemnization of Matrimony the Clerke shall receive 4d and noe more unless it be given in curtesy.

For digging and berying a grave for any person under 10 years of age he shall demand 6d and noe more, and if the party buryed be above 10 yeares of age he shall demand 1s 0d and noe more.

These continued to be the basic duties of a Parish Clerk, but some had a much wider range of accomplishments. John Hopkins, a parish clerk in Salisbury at the end of the eighteenth century, inserted an advertisement in the local newspaper which gives some indication of the range of his talents and functions:

John Hopkins, parish clerk and undertaker, sells epitaphs of all sorts and prices. Shaves neat, and plays the bassoon. Teeth drawn and the Salisbury Journal read gratis every Sunday morning at eight. A school for psalmody every Thursday evening, when my son, born blind, will play the fiddle. Specimen epitaph on my wife:—

> My wife ten years, not much to my ease,
> But now she is dead, in caelo quies'.

Congregational singing and the use of choirs and musicians became increasingly popular in parish churches during the eighteenth century. Generally it was the metrical version of the psalms by Tate and Brady, easily committed to memory and simple to sing, but hardly doing justice to the poetry of the originals—

> As pants the hart for cooling streams
> When heated in the chase,
> So longs my soul O God for thee,
> And thy refreshing grace.

or

> Lord, hear the voice of my complaint,
> To my request give ear.
> Preserve my soul from cruel foes,
> And free my soul from fear.

At first singing was started by the parish clerk using a pitch-pipe or tuning fork, but increasingly during this period churches obtained small

21. *A Country Church Interior, J. Wright 1790* An informative drawing of an unrestored church interior of the eighteenth century; note the musicians and choir in the west gallery, the 'three-decker' pulpit and sounding-board, the monuments, hatchments and tattered banners, and the cluttered pews with an obviously ill-behaved rustic congregation.

22. *Dancing around the Church, W. W. Wheatley, 1848* This remarkable picture shows the ancient annual ceremony of 'clipping the church' or dancing around it; the origins of this practice are no doubt pre-Christian for its purpose was to create a magical chain against the powers of evil and to drive away the devil. The picture was painted at Rode, Somerset, on Shrove Tuesday night, 1848.

groups of musicians to accompany the services on a variety of instruments, strings, woodwinds and brass. Churchwardens' accounts provide abundant details of this process. For example, the accounts for the parish of Kentisbeare, Devon contain the following references to the purchase of musical instruments:

    1776 a bass viol
    1787 a hautboy
    1794 a bassoon
    1807 a flute
    1810 a German flute, a clarinet

Other accounts also provide references to serpents, fiddles, oboes, trumpets and cornets, as well as to the purchase of sheet-music both for the instrumentalists and for the singers. The singers were dressed in their ordinary clothing during this period; not until the nineteenth century did surpliced choirs appear in parish churches. In the late eighteenth and early nineteenth centuries barrel-organs became popular for providing musical accompaniment to the services, though inevitably their repertoire was limited. Their popularity can be judged from the number which survive, especially in East Anglia. Later the harmonium was introduced and finally the organ made its appearance and rapidly found favour in parish churches, appealing particularly to the desire of the clergy for 'seemliness' and decency, and deposing the other more attractive instruments of music. The dull uniformity of organ music is not the least of the unfortunate innovations which have been imposed upon English parish churches.

An example of the way in which the village musicians of the eighteenth century were replaced during the early nineteenth century by an organ, the sort of development that was occurring throughout the country during the period, can be seen from the churchwardens' accounts of Crewkerne, Somerset. Throughout the eighteenth and early nineteenth centuries there are occasional references in the accounts to small sums being spent on the maintenance of the musical instruments of the church, among them a violin, bass viol, and bassoon. This continued until 1823 when the curate, Dr Robert Ashe, presented the church with a new London-made organ. The musicians' services were evidently dispensed with immediately, but the churchwardens soon found that the new method of providing music was much more expensive than the old. An annual salary of £25 had to be paid to Mrs Budden the organist for her services, and a further £2 a year to the organ-blower. In 1826 Mrs Budden was succeeded by John Summerhays at an annual salary of £30 per annum. By his generous and no doubt kindly meant gift Dr Ashe had vastly increased the Crewkerne churchwardens' expenditure on music. The village bands gradually disappeared from parish churches during the nineteenth century, though a few survived in remote places into the twentieth century.

There are few descriptions of the atmosphere and character of ordinary parish-church services during the Georgian period. The general impression that remains is of the predictability of the Prayer Book service, of the length and dullness of the sermon which seems from the many published examples which survive to have been couched in terms far above the heads of most congregations, and of the prevailing somnolence of the occasion. It is not without significance that eighteenth-century churches employed 'wakers' to patrol the aisles and rouse the sleepers. For example at Shefford, Buckinghamshire, in 1825 James Haddow was paid £2 12s 0d per annum for winding the church clock, cleaning the church, and for walking around during the services to prod the sleepers. The atmosphere is perhaps best recaptured by Thomas Hardy's lines

> On afternoons of drowsy calm,
> We stood in the panelled pew,
> Singing one-voiced a Tate and Brady psalm
> To the tune of Cambridge New.

This, however, was what most clergy regarded as desirable for the church services; dullness was not the enemy to be feared so much as 'enthusiasm' or fanaticism on the one hand, or anything which smacked of 'popery' on the other. It was against this that the Methodists rebelled and eventually separated from the Church.

Not many parish churches during the eighteenth century approached the ideal situation of everyone in the community attending the regular services for, as well as Dissenters, there were many who seldom came to church. But few people could escape the religious ministrations of their parish church altogether. Baptism was regarded by most people as essential, both for the child's physical and spiritual well-being; for it was steadfastly believed in country parishes that a baby would hardly 'thrive' without the assistance of this Sacrament. Equally, most parishioners were obliged to resort to their parish church for marriage and few could escape from being buried in the churchyard and in accordance with the service in the Book of Common Prayer. Eighteenth-century christenings were frequently celebrated with great gusto and feasting, especially among wealthier families; funerals ranged from the miserable interment of paupers buried at the expense of the parish and in as cheap a style as possible, to the lavish affairs of the gentry whose cortège was accompanied by long processions of mourners and upon whose burial and memorial very large sums were commonly spent. Weddings, too, varied greatly, and not all were joyous events. Some couples were forced into marriage by their families, who were concerned more about matters of inheritance, lands, property and connections than with any mutual attraction between the parties. Other marriages were insisted upon by parish officials whose only concern was to save the expense to the parish of an illegitimate child. The Rev. James Woodeforde of Weston Longueville (Norfolk) confided to his diary in 1787 his uneasiness at being called upon to conduct such marriages:

Rode to Ringland this morning and married one Robe. Astick and Elizabeth Howlett by Licence . . . the Man being in Custody, the Woman being with Child by him. The Man was a long time before he could be prevailed on to marry her when in the Church Yard; and at the Altar behaved very unbecoming. It is cruel that any Person should be compelled by Law to marry. . . . It is very disagreeable to me to marry such Persons.

The accounts for many such marriages are to be found in parish records. For example at Blandford Forum in 1780 Mary Harvey had named John Hardy as the father of her illegitimate child. The overseers' accounts give the following details of the mixture of bribery and coercion which had to be used before the marriage took place and a potential burden lifted from the parish:

Licence to marry John Hardy	£2 os 6d
To John Hardy as a premium	£2 2s od
A gold ring	7s 6d
Marriage	7s 6d
Expense at White Hart	£1 15s od
To two men guarding John Hardy two nights and part of two days	8s od

The parish church also continued to touch life at many points not purely ecclesiastical, and this was especially true of rural parishes. In many places the musicians and the choir were an important feature of the social life of the community as well as of the church services, and were in demand for weddings and other celebrations. The bell-ringers also formed an important section of the local community. It is impossible to read the churchwardens' accounts of any parish from the fifteenth century onwards without being quickly made aware of the importance of the bells, for they were always expensive to maintain and demanded constant expenditure upon their upkeep. The fact that the necessary large sums continued to be provided, and that during the eighteenth century new bells were added to many peals, is in itself evidence of the continuing popularity of bells and bell-ringing. They were rung not only to summon people to church, but for weddings and to give warnings of fire or other disasters, to celebrate victories, to mark occasions such as the monarch's birthday, Oak Apple Day, Guy Fawkes Day and other festivities, and even to ward off violent storms and thunder. They were tolled for funerals or as a 'passing Bell' at the time of death of any inhabitant, and as a rising bell and a curfew. In towns like Bath no visitor could arrive with coach and horses except he was welcomed by a peal of the church bells, a privilege for which he would of course be expected to pay.

In a few places traditions and ceremonies from an earlier period lingered on, such as at Marnhull in Dorset where it had long been the custom by the terms of an ancient charity for the parson to distribute bread, cheese and beer for consumption in the church on Easter Day: as much beer was provided as could be brewed from a bushell of malt, and as much bread as could be made from four bushells of wheat, the bread being 'good white bread' and not 'ordinary'; 110 lb. of 'ordinary' (i.e. skimmed milk) cheese was provided or 100 lb. of better quality cheese. The bread and cheese was cut into pieces and, together with the beer, brought into the church every year after Evening Prayer on Easter Day by the parson.

At Kidlington, Oxfordshire, a medieval bequest which had originally been intended for the benefit of those who attended Midnight Mass on Christmas Eve was continued. By the terms of this bequest the rent from certain lands in the parish was used to provide a breakfast consisting of three-quarters of an ox and large quantities of bread and beer, and although Midnight Mass had ceased at the Reformation the breakfast was still provided at the unlikely hour of 3.00 a.m. on Christmas morning. The result of this curiously timed feast was to make many of the inhabitants so drunk that they were unfit to attend church at any time on Christmas Day. But such survivals were by the eighteenth century no more than curiosities; much more important in most parishes was the intimate involvement of the parish church and its officers in the distribution of charity and poor relief. A remarkably large number of small charities existed, providing for the distribution of money, bread, coals and clothing to the poor, or for the apprenticing of poor children, particularly to those who regularly attended church or who were not in regular receipt of poor relief. The evidence for these charities may be observed on the boards which are still displayed in many churches giving details of parochial bequests and benefactors. The great majority of these were administered and distributed by the clergy and churchwardens or by the overseers of the poor, and were centred upon the parish church. Further evidence of these benefactions survives in the 'dole cupboards' or receptacles for loaves of bread or other provisions which survive in some churches. Although overseers of the poor had been appointed annually in each parish since 1601, the churchwardens still performed a number of functions in connection with the relief of poverty and the distribution of private charity, using offerings of money made on Sacrament Sundays to buy coal and food for the poor, or to relieve travellers or those claiming to have 'had greate losse by fire' and similar misfortunes. This sort of overlapping of functions was common in English villages, for private charity and philanthropy was encouraged by the Church and for long continued to be important in the relief of poverty alongside the more formal provision of the State with its compulsory poor rates. Nor should the private benevolence of the clergy be forgotten, for whatever other shortcomings they may have had, many of the clergy were extremely kind and helpful towards their parishioners in times of trouble, as published clerical diaries such as those of James Woodforde and William Cole show.

The Church was also directly involved in the life of agricultural communities in various ways. The incumbent himself was often intimately concerned, especially if he was farming his own glebe; he depended for a major part of his livelihood upon the tithes of farmers, and in many parishes he continued to be responsible for providing a bull and a boar for the use of his parishioners. As during previous centuries, work on their glebe farms occupied the time of many clergymen. They would have immediately recognised the description of Parson Trulliber in Fielding's *Joseph Andrews*,

stript into his waistcoat, with an apron on, and a pail in his hand, just come from serving his hogs; for Mr. Trulliber was a parson on Sundays, but all the other six might properly be called a farmer.

A few of the clergy were active in promoting agricultural improvements, advocating new methods and crops, such as turnips and potatoes, or urging forward the progress of enclosure, experimenting with allotments for labourers, model housing etc. Notable among such men was Jethro Tull; another example was John Trist, vicar of Veryan in Cornwall from 1782 to 1829. He was involved in various agricultural improvements and played a major part in drawing up the *General View of the Agriculture of the County of Cornwall* for the Board of Agriculture in 1811. This contains Trist's plan for a labourer's cottage, circular in plan, which, he claimed, was cheap and easy to build and convenient to live in; four of these 'round houses' remain and are still lived in at Veryan. A great many other clergy were similarly involved in agricultural improvements.

The collection of tithes, although it brought the clergy into contact with their parishioners, created inestimable difficulties and ill-feeling. Until the whole system was reformed in 1836, tithes remained legally payable in kind, and although in many parishes they had for long been commuted into money payments, the methods of assessment still gave fruitful opportunities for dispute; and there remained numerous parishes where the clergy continued the troublesome business of collecting their tithes in kind. Constantly they had to face the dilemma of whether to make themselves unpopular and their spiritual work more difficult by insisting in full on their just rights, or to allow themselves to be defrauded in order to keep the peace in their parishes. As a correspondent to the *Monthly Magazine* wrote in 1798,

Very few clergymen in England who take their tithes in kind retain the good opinion of their parishioners, and therefore have but little prospect of ministering to their religious improvement.

Another way in which the parish church was closely involved with the farming community was through the churchwardens' responsibility for the control of vermin in the parish. Thus a steady stream of persons arrived at country churches bringing with them innumerable dead sparrows and other small birds, rooks, hawks, foxes, badgers, otters and hedgehogs, in order to claim the bounty payable by the churchwardens. Year after year churchwardens' accounts record the payments made for these creatures. For example at Westoning, Bedfordshire, in 1743 they paid a bounty on 138 dozen sparrows, and at Cerne Abbas, Dorset, in 1753 the wardens paid for 85 dozen sparrows, 37 hedgehogs, 9 polecats, 9 stoats and 4 foxes. At Thorncombe, Dorset, in 1751 a parish meeting agreed the following scale of payments:

Michevious farments and other birds to be paid for as Follows:

First, to pay for the heads of Foxes							one shilling each
Item ,, ,, ,, ,,				,,	,, Martins		,, ,, ,,
,, ,, ,, ,, ,,				,,	,, Pole Cats		4d. per head
,, ,, ,, ,, ,,				,,	,, Stoats		2d. ,, ,,
,, ,, ,, ,, ,,				,,	,, Kites & Hawks		4d. ,, ,,
,, ,, ,, ,, ,,				,,	,, Jays & Whoops		4d. ,, ,,
,, ,, ,, ,, ,,				,,	,, Crows & Magepyes		1d. ,, ,,
,, ,, ,, ,, ,,				,,	,, Sparrows		2d. per Dozen.

In some parishes, meetings of various sorts continued to be held in the churches. The overseers of the poor, the supervisors of the highways and other parish officials continued to use the church, particularly in country parishes. For example, the parish vestry meetings at Bitton, Gloucestershire, were held regularly in the parish church throughout this period, and considered topics as various as the appointment of parish officers, the care of the poor, the apprenticing of pauper children, the conduct of the parish poor-house, the repair of the church, care of the churchyard, maintenance of the bells and administration of the parish lands and charities. The church services were also used as an opportunity for giving out notices on all sorts of secular subjects such as poor-rate assessments or appeals for news of strayed sheep and cattle, and the church porch was the recognised place for the display of proclamations and advertisements. The parish church at Molland in north Devon still has the notices giving detailed information concerning the action to be taken if the Napoleonic army landed, the places to which cattle and sheep should be driven, and where the parishioners should seek refuge.

During the eighteenth century the parish church and churchyard assumed a new role for many people. This was as a place to display memorials to the departed members of their families. Previously the practice of erecting elaborate tombs, headstones, wall-tablets and the like had been largely confined to the wealthy gentry families; now the middle classes as well as the clergy eagerly seized the opportunity for the ostentatious display of wealth, family pride and grief, by raising the enormous monuments and laudatory tablets which still remain a major feature of most parish churches. In addition, the gentry continued the practice of displaying in the churches the diamond-shaped hatchments bearing the coat of arms of deceased members of their families, as well as erecting ever-larger and more costly memorials.

A number of churches maintained stocks of books, and thus constituted the only source of serious reading matter in most parishes. In town churches like All Saints', Northampton, Boston and Grantham, Lincolnshire, All Saints', Bristol or St John's, Bedford, there were notable libraries, and many smaller churches had fine collections of books. During the eighteenth century the practice of holding Sunday schools in the churches began, a movement which was to gain momentum in the next century and was to play an important part in educational advance. This subject, together with the other changes and developments in parish churches and church-life during the nineteenth century will be discussed in the next chapter.

7. Revival, rebuilding and restoration

The nineteenth century witnessed change and revival in every aspect of the life and work of the Anglican church; there was a new vigour and a new sense of the responsibilities of their calling among the clergy. The most obvious sign of the resurgence was the massive increase in the number of parish churches, especially in the new and rapidly-growing towns, as the Church strove valiantly but unsuccessfully to keep pace with the expanding population of the country. Between 1801 and 1851 the population of England and Wales doubled, increasing from 9 million to 18 million, and by 1911 the figure had doubled again to 36 million. Most of this growth occurred in the towns, especially in the new towns where the provision of parish churches was already woefully inadequate at the beginning of the nineteenth century. The organisation of the Church of England was best suited to a predominantly rural society, and the framework of dioceses and parishes was ill-fitted to cope with such a population-explosion. 'The parochial system', wrote the devoted layman and philanthropist Lord Shaftesbury in 1855, 'is, no doubt, a beautiful thing in theory, and is of great value in small rural districts; but in the large towns it is a mere shadow and a name.' Even where enough churches existed it was not always easy for newcomers or casual visitors to secure a seat, for, as was shown in the last chapter, many pews were rented and were regarded as private property by those who had paid for the right to sit in them, and who had frequently rebuilt, decorated and adorned them to their own taste and for their own comfort. Joseph Leech, the editor of a Bristol newspaper, published a long series of articles on local churches during the 1840s, under the pseudonym 'Church-Goer', and wrote in 1847 that

. . . every pew is like a preserve: you must not put your hand on the first door you meet, for if this green cloth lining, these soft cushions, these rich carpets, these mohair hassocks, these morocco-bound, gilt-edged Prayer Books and Bibles lying about, be not sufficient to protect the seat from rash intrusion, you must be very dull or very daring indeed . . .

When Leech visited Yatton Church (then in Somerset, now Avon) he could not find a vacant pew and was obliged to sit with the poor on a bench at the back of the church. It was so unusual to see a well-dressed man occupying such a seat that '. . . even the school children who, headed by the master carrying a music book in his hand, entered in a long file . . . and . . . came pat, pat, clatter in their wooden shoes up the aisles, immediately descried the stranger, and looked over their snub noses at me as if I had two heads'.

Gradually the practice of renting pews and seats in churches was abandoned, but it died out slowly and in some places survived well into the twentieth century. To make up for the loss of revenue from pew-rents churchwardens turned increasingly to taking collections from congregations during the services, and by the end of the nineteenth century this custom had become almost universal.

Even without the problem of private pews however, the churches could accommodate hardly more than half the people, and the problem got worse as the population increased. In 1801 there were seats for some 58 out of every 100 people: by 1851 only about 45 per cent could be accommodated. The figures for many of the larger and new towns, where the appalling living-conditions and attendant social problems meant that the ministrations of the Church were most urgently needed, were much worse. In Leeds, for example, during the early nineteenth century there were church places for only 5 per cent of the population; and in Bradford as late as 1858 there were only 1,400 church seats for a population of 78,000, and only 200 of these seats were free, the rest having been let to private individuals. When Charles Lowder was instituted to the tough London parish of St Georges-in-the-East in 1842 he was almost overwhelmed by the problems he found there, and not least by the fact that crowded into the slums and alleys of his parish were more than 38,000 people. Many other clergy in town parishes faced a similar situation.

Nonetheless, the church did strive manfully to keep pace with the changing circumstances, especially from the 1830s when the revival stimulated by the Evangelical clergy on the one hand and by the 'Oxford Movement' led by such men as Pusey, Keble and Newman, on the other, began to make itself felt, and when the demand on all sides for reforms in the Church as well as in the State had become irresistible. The outward and visible signs of the change can best be seen in the figures for church building. The process was given a great impetus at the start by a Government grant of a million pounds for church building in 1818. Ostensibly this was a thank-offering for victory at Waterloo and resulted in the so-called 'Waterloo' churches; more realistically it was an attempt to provide some civilizing influence in the barren wastes of the mushrooming towns and new suburbs. For whatever the motivation of the more zealous of the clergy, the government was largely impelled by the hope that the new churches might serve to check the violence and lawlessness among the lower classes in the crowded slums; as Charles Blomfield, the reforming Bishop of London put it in 1836, church-building was 'a work of prudence no less than charity'. The following statistics tell their own story of increasing zeal and endeavour within the Church, and of a staggeringly large programme of church-building.

ANGLICAN CHURCH BUILDING, 1801–75

Quinquennia	New churches	Churches rebuilt	Total churches consecrated
1801–05	10	7	17
1806–10	18	8	26
1811–15	27	12	39
1816–20	43	14	57
1821–25	97	33	130
1826–30	138	40	178
1831–35	154	48	202
1836–40	360	38	398
1841–45	401	78	479
1846–50	358	92	450
1851–55	342	77	419
1856–60	312	89	401
1861–65	364	156	520
1866–70	427	163	590
1871–75	356	152	508

(The above figures are taken from A. D. Gilbert, *Religion and Society in Industrial England*, 1976, p. 130.)

In all parts of the country the number of new churches built during the nineteenth century was impressive. There were 106 new churches built in the diocese of Oxford during the episcopate of Bishop Wilberforce, 1845–69; in the diocese of Manchester Bishop Lee consecrated 110 new churches during the period 1848–69. Even in the predominantly rural diocese of Gloucester 54 new churches were consecrated between 1832 and 1864, and in Hampshire during the same period there were 82 new churches and in Surrey 87.

In 1836 the Ecclesiastical Commission was appointed by Parliament and began the herculean task of reforming the Church's financial and administrative structure. Gradually things improved. In 1854 G. A. Selwyn, who had been a bishop in New Zealand, returned to England and, preaching at Cambridge, was able to say 'a great and visible change has taken place in the 13 years since I left England. It is now a very rare thing to see a careless clergyman, a neglected parish or a desecrated church', although nonetheless, he was still at pains to draw attention to the continuing existence in the great towns of 'the dark masses of our uninstructed people'.

As with so much else in nineteenth-century England, the Church's renewed concern and revitalised outlook operated through a mixture of private and public benevolence, and essentially through societies and committees. The names and foundation-dates of the societies alone provide a measure of the revival. The 'National Society for the Education of the Poor in the Principles of the Established Church' was founded in 1811, and within two years of its creation was catering for 40,000 children. It is remembered in the name 'National School' which is still to be seen on countless school-buildings. The Church Building Society was formed in 1818; the Church Pastoral Aid Society 1836; the Additional Curates Society 1837. In their involvement in education during the nineteenth century the parish churches of England made an incalculable impact upon society. Victorian England was nurtured in Sunday schools and Church day-schools. Sunday schools started in the later eighteenth century, and under the dedicated direction of such people as Robert Raikes and Hannah More and countless other devoted teachers, such schools for long gave to many of their scholars all the education they ever received. The Bible was used as the main subject of study, but from this came reading and writing, and in some places arithmetic was also taught. Many Sunday schools were held in the churches themselves, and lasted for most of each Sunday, with necessary breaks for the services. In Nottingham in 1802 some 1,860 children were in some form of Sunday school, and by 1834 this figure had risen to at least 7,000; in 1851 there were 38 Sunday schools in the town with a total of 9,000 children. By 1887 more than two million children in England and Wales were attending Church of England Sunday schools, and only slightly fewer were to be found at the various Nonconformist Sunday schools. The Church's part in day-schools also grew rapidly after the founding of the National Society in 1811, and by 1831 there were 400,000 scholars in Anglican day-schools. The number of Church schools continued to increase until the State became involved in the provision of schools in 1870. In education, however, as in so much else affecting the religious life of Victorian England, the subject was bedevilled by the rivalry and bitter disputes between the Anglican and nonconformist churches, resulting in local feuds, duplication of efforts and a mutual antagonism which could hardly be called Christian.

VICTORIAN RESTORATION

The concern for new churches was accompanied by a new care for existing churches, which unfortunately led to the wholesale 'restorations' of the Victorian period. Few English parish churches escaped these well-intentioned attempts to make them worthy of the new standards of worship, and enormous sums of money were spent to rid them of what were regarded by zealous reformers as the superfluous and inappropriate accretions of the centuries. There were undoubtedly many churches which were in urgent need of restoration and of overhaul, and it is easy to find examples of churches suffering from neglect and decay during the early nineteenth century. But these were a minority, and few churches required the drastic treatment accorded to both structure and furnishings by the Victorian restorers. To church restorers, such as Sir Gilbert Scott, G. E. Street, J. P. Seddon, B. Ferrey and many others, there was a specifically Christian style of architecture, and they believed that its highest expression had been achieved during the thirteenth and fourteenth centuries; their endeavour was therefore to *restore* as far as possible the features of the church at that period, and to clear away all the additions which centuries of Christian use had made to the buildings. In their enthusiasm and piety the Victorian restorers saw in the form and design of the medieval churches a symbolism which would have astonished the medieval masons who were concerned only to meet the practical needs of contemporary congregations and clergy. The unfortunate result was that the stonework of churches was ruthlessly scraped and re-chiselled, new highly-coloured and garish stained glass was provided for the windows, and often the stonework and tracery of the windows was also changed; the plaster on interior walls was removed, and with it went seventeenth- and eighteenth-century texts as well as any underlying medieval wall-paintings. So thorough were many restorations that they involved the virtual demolition and re-building of the church so that it might accord with some theory of ecclesiastical 'correctness'. Sir Gilbert Scott removed a pre-Conquest arch at Godalming (Surrey) and substituted a new arch in what he thought was the more 'correct' style of the thirteenth century. At Stoke d'Abernon in the same county the pre-Conquest church was totally altered by a destructive 'restoration' in 1866. A contemporary illustration of the 'restoration' of Broadwindsor church (Dorset) in 1868 shows that only the tower was left standing and that the walls were almost entirely rebuilt. Hundreds of churches underwent similar drastic and often totally unnecessary treatment.

Furnishings not in accord with the restorer's conception of 'correctness' were also ruthlessly removed. Screens, 'three-decker' pulpits, high pews and many post-Reformation furnishings were swept away, often in favour of new pine furniture from approved modern-church suppliers. Particular care was lavished upon the chancel which was frequently raised so that it was necessary to ascend two or three steps from the nave. The altar could thus dominate the whole church, and an elaborate marble reredos replaced the Creed, Lord's Prayer and Commandments which had previously been written on the east wall. Floors were tiled, new lecterns, pulpits, litany-desks were provided; choir-stalls were placed in the chancel and the choir brought out of the west gallery which was generally removed during restorations. Open seats or chairs were substituted for the old box-pews. Many memorials and monuments were also removed and either disappeared or were relegated to dark and inaccessible corners. Only in those comparatively few churches which escaped the attention of the restorers is it possible to realise the scale of the destruction involved. In churches like Cameley (Avon), Molland (Devon), Icklingham All Saints (Suffolk), Chaldon (Surrey), Ranworth (Norfolk) and others which can still be found in all parts of the country, it is possible to see the sort of richness and interest which was a common feature of the pre-Victorian parish church. Doubtless the unrestored interiors of many churches were untidy and inconvenient, the result of haphazard additions to the furnishings over several centuries, but the sweeping restorations of the nineteenth century effectively completed the work of the reformers of the sixteenth and seventeenth centuries, and deprived succeeding generations of much beauty and interest.

Alongside the drastic alteration in the appearance of countless English parish churches came great changes in the conduct of public worship, for many of the clergy, inspired by the teachings of the Oxford Movement, began to restore ritual, vestments and other accessories to the services which had not been seen in English churches since the Reformation. The more extreme caused great offence by the use of chasubles, albs, copes and birettas and by the introduction of tapers, incense, the reserved sacrament and other features associated in the popular mind with Catholicism. Such innovations led to unseemly public protests and occasionally to violence in churches and to cases before the ecclesiastical and secular courts. But even moderate clergy began to introduce a cross and candles on the altar, and a surpliced-choir situated in the chancel. The latter led in turn to much greater emphasis on music and singing and to a demand both for anthems for the choir and for hymns for the congregation. *Hymns Ancient and Modern*, which was to become the most widely used hymn-book in the country, was first published in 1860 though new editions and enlargements rapidly followed. The result of surpliced-choirs, greater use of music (especially organ music), and congregational participation in hymn-singing was that services even in small country churches took on a completely new appearance and atmosphere, quite different from the somnolent worship of the previous century. Gone were the village musicians in the west gallery, their violins, serpents, bass recorders, flutes and other instruments replaced by the organ; gone were the Tate and Brady metrical psalms, announced and led by the parish clerk. The 'three-decker pulpit' was replaced by a reading-desk, lecturn and modern pulpit, and the surpliced-choir in the chancel concentrated the attention of worshippers upon the east end of the church and upon the altar in a way which was quite unknown in the eighteenth century. Communion services became more frequent, monthly or even weekly instead of the eighteenth-century norm of three or four times a year, and the number of communicants increased greatly. The introduction of Harvest Festival services during the later nineteenth century created another extremely popular community event, especially in rural parishes, and led to a widespread revival of the practice of decorating the churches, not only with the fruits of the harvest, but also at Christmas and Easter.

The nineteenth century also saw a greater sense of responsibility and dedication among the clergy. Francis Kilvert, whose published diary gives an invaluable record of church-life in a country parish, was curate at Langley Burrell in Wiltshire during the years 1872 to 1876; there he conducted Matins and Evensong each with a sermon every Sunday, and also a Sunday School morning and afternoon; Holy Communion was celebrated on one Sunday a month after Matins, and also on the great festivals; there were also services on Ash Wednesday and Ascension Day. Kilvert visited the sick, involved himself fully in parish life, taught in the village school every day, and gave evening lectures on a great range of different subjects to his parishioners every Wednesday. There were also occasional bible-readings, communicants' meetings and confirmation classes. Kilvert's busy routine and involvement in community life could have been matched by hundreds of his contemporaries, but would have amazed their eighteenth-century predecessors.

THE DECLINE IN CHURCH-GOING

There can be no doubt that many of the clergy made tireless efforts to involve their church in every aspect of community life during the nineteenth century. The proliferation of church schools, Sunday schools, clubs, guilds, fellowships and societies of all sorts attached to or run by the parish churches bears witness to their endeavours, and Victorian society would have been infinitely poorer without such organisations. Parish life became much more vigorous and there was a renewed effort to involve the laity. During the later nineteenth century many parishes saw the introduction of a parish magazine which, together with tracts and other publications, and regular parish meetings on weekdays for bible study, prayer, discussion and worship added greatly to corporate life, as did such institutions as the Mothers' Union, the Girls' Friendly Society, Young Men's Clubs, parish libraries and reading-rooms and a lively social life centred upon the parish church. But the results of the 1851 census revealed in painful detail that the church had not succeeded in securing or recapturing the allegiance of large sections of society and particularly of the urban working-classes. As well as the census of population which was taken in 1851 a census was also taken of places of religious worship and of the number of people who attended them on Sunday 30 March. This was the only occasion on which such an enquiry was made, and the results came as a sad shock to many churchmen, for they revealed in cold statistics the extent to which the Church of England had lost the loyalty of working people, and how few attended any form of religious worship. Of the 18 million people in England and Wales, only 7 million were shown as having attended a place of religious worship on 30 March 1851, and the true number was probably a good deal lower because many of those who did attend were counted at both morning and evening services. But even worse for the Church of England was the fact that only some $3\frac{1}{2}$ million attended an Anglican church; and the figure for the larger towns was pitifully small, a fact masked in the overall statistics by the comparatively large attendances in rural areas and the small country towns. In only six out of the 37 largest northern industrial towns was the national average

23. *The Village Choir, Thomas Webster* A somewhat romanticised picture of
musicians and singers in the west gallery.

24. *The Serpent* A popular instrument with church musicians during the eighteenth and early nineteenth centuries. This instrument was in use at Chew Stoke, Avon, until the 1850s.

25. *Interior of Barrel Organ, Isle Abbots, Somerset* Such organs, with their limited repertoire of tunes, were often the first replacement for the village musicians; later during the 19th century harmoniums and finally pipe organs were purchased and installed in almost every parish.

of 58 per cent church attendance reached in 1851, and in Bethnal Green, London, out of 90,000 people only 6,000 attended church.

The figures of the 1851 Census confronted the leaders of the Church inescapably with the stark fact, which many had already recognised, that they had lost a significant proportion of the people. As Flora Thompson was later to write of the 1880s in *Lark Rise to Candleford*:

If Lark Rise people had been asked their religion, the answer of nine out of ten would have been 'Church of England', for practically all of them were christened, married and buried as such, although in adult life few went to church between the baptisms of their offspring.

In some villages church attendance by the labourers was insisted upon by the gentry and farmers; in others constant church attenders had preference for charities and minor jobs. Others attended through long use and because it was the accepted custom to do so. Typical of many farm labourers was the father of Joseph Arch, the agricultural trade unionist, who lived in the Warwickshire village of Barford. He was regular in church attendance, and Joseph Arch later wrote of him:

I suppose he kept on going because he had always been accustomed to go, so to church he went. And there were other working men like him in that.

When such men and their families moved to the new towns, however, their church attendance often lapsed in the new environment. It was, in general and in spite of many exceptions, only among the upper and middle classes of society that church-going remained as an accepted norm in many of the new or greatly expanded towns of Victorian England. The idea that Victorian churches were full or that church-going was the accepted normal practice is a myth. Nonetheless, there were many parishes, especially in rural areas, where the figures for church-attendance were very high indeed and where the parish church continued to occupy a central position in the social, educational, charitable and recreational life of the community comparable to the situation in the Middle Ages, and where weekly attendance at the parish church remained the principal regular social event in the community. The vital concern of many sections of Victorian society with religion and religious observance can still be seen in the churches, missions, schools, hospitals, orphanages and many other institutions which they built and in the number of religious societies which they founded.

In many country parishes the old leadership of society by squire and parson continued unchanged throughout the nineteenth century. The right of presentation of the incumbent was vested in local landowners and the clergy remained as an essential and accepted part of the social order. Even the most ardent reformers among the bishops accepted the need for this link between church and state. Sydney Smith, who was later to become a canon of St Pauls, satirised Bishop Blomfield's instructions to his clergy during 1825 in lines which sum up, admirably if unkindly, one continuing aspect of Anglicanism:

> Hunt not, fish not, shoot not;
> Dance not, fiddle not, flute not;
> But before all things, its my particular desire,
> That once at least in every week, you take
> Your dinner with the Squire.

Several of the reforms of the nineteenth century had the indirect effect of reducing the area of daily life in which the church and its officers were involved. The Poor Law Amendment Act of 1834 took many of the responsibilities for the poor away from the parishes and from the parish officials; the Tithe Commutation Act of 1836 created a regular and more satisfactory basis for the payment of tithes, but incidentally destroyed the ancient direct contact between the incumbent and the tithe-payers, a contact which had frequently been far from harmonious but which at least reminded both sides of the others' existence. The wide-ranging powers of the church courts over the laity relating to such things as the supervision of morals, testamentary matters, marriages, adultery, libel and slander, gradually declined through lack of regular use and were finally abolished in 1860. In 1868 the ancient compulsory church rates which had created so much ill-feeling among nonconformists were abolished; and in 1894 the Local Government Act set up parish councils which, unlike the older vestry meetings, were quite separate from the parish church and its officers.

The Victorian sense of propriety also tended to dissociate parish churches from some of the older, traditional community activities which were no longer regarded by the clergy as quite 'proper', but in which the church had hitherto been closely involved. Such events included wakes and feasts on the patronal festivals, Christmas, Easter and Whitsun jollities and revels, Friendly Society annual processions, bell-ringing contests, and such ancient folk-customs as those of Boxing Day, Plough Monday (the first Monday after Epiphany), or May Day and ceremonies with their roots in a long-forgotten, pre-Christian past such as 'clipping' or dancing around the church on Shrove Tuesday (*see* illustration no. 22, dated as late as 1848). . . . There is no doubt that such events had frequently been accompanied by excessive drinking and unseemly behaviour, but by withdrawing its countenance from them and attempting to substitute less robust activities such as garden fêtes and tea parties, the Victorian church undoubtedly lost another important contact with community life.

After the alarming church-attendance figures of 1851, further shocks were in store for the churches, for in 1859 Darwin published his *Origin of Species*, to be followed in 1871 by *The Descent of Man*, and many churchmen saw the whole foundation of their belief under attack. Theological critics were also sowing the seeds of scepticism about some parts of the Bible, and the gap between science and religion was rapidly becoming a chasm. Charles Booth's survey of London life during the years 1897–1900 revealed that no more than 20 per cent of the population of the capital attended any place of religious worship.

It is not the intention of this book to pursue the story of the church's role in society into the twentieth century, or to chart the continuing decline in church attendances. Nor is this the place to discuss the immensely important question that now confronts both church and society of how to care for the large number of church-buildings which are no longer required for worship or where the congregation is inadequate to maintain the building. But in spite of the manifold contemporary problems of the Church, there are heartening signs that in many places parish churches are beginning once more to play a significant role in the social as well as in the religious life of the communities which they serve. During the nineteenth century and for long afterwards, secular use of parish churches was unusual and it was seldom considered proper to use the buildings for anything other than religious worship. The contemporary efforts to find new and additional uses for parish churches as social and recreational centres, and to use them for parish meetings, concerts, plays and assemblies of all sorts as well as for services, are hopeful signs that a continuing and worthwhile secular as well as religious function can once again be found for English parish churches.

Those who raised the money and organised the building of the great heritage of English medieval parish churches would have seen little incongruity in their use for concerts, plays, conferences and exhibitions alongside their essential role as places of worship. But above all they would have emphasised that the buildings must be used to the greater glory of

God, and must serve as visible daily reminders of Man's relationship to the Almighty. The constant, recurring ideal of church builders throughout the centuries is admirably summed up in the words of those who planned and built on a lavish scale the extravagant and expensive Gothic chapel for Lancing College in 1854: 'It will lead men to ask what can have been the inducements which have called forth so large a sacrifice of money and of labour, for which there can be no adequate worldly return, and in that inquiry find the true solution.'

Select Bibliography

The following bibliography lists a few of the most helpful general books out of the vast literature on church architecture and social history. There are, however, few books which deal specifically with the *use* of church buildings and the part they played in community life, and most information on this subject is confined to articles in specialist journals or in the Proceedings of the various county Archaeological and Record Societies.

W. ADDISON: *The English Country Parson*, 1947

G. W. ADDLESHAW AND F. ETCHELLS: *The Architectural Setting of Anglican Worship*, 1948

M. D. ANDERSON: *History and Imagery in British Churches*, 1971

J. BERESFORD (ed.): *The Diary of a Country Parson: The Rev. James Woodforde*, 1924–31

B. F. L. CLARKE: *Church Builders of the Nineteenth Century*, 1938

G. H. COOK: *The English Medieval Parish Church*, 1954

G. H. COOK: *Medieval Chantries and Chantry Chapels*, 1947

P. COWLEY: *The Church Houses*, 1970

J. C. COX: *Churchwardens' Accounts*, 1913

J. C. COX: *The English Parish Church*, 1914

S. J. CURTIS: *History of Education in Great Britain*, 1967

H. DAVIES: *The English Free Churches*, 1963

J. G. DAVIES: *The Secular Use of Church Buildings*, 1968

A. G. DICKENS: *The English Reformation*, 1964

R. W. DUNNING (ed.): *Christianity in Somerset*, 1976

MARGARET GELLING: *Signposts to the Past: Place-names and the history of England*, 1978

A. D. GILBERT: *Religion and Society in Industrial England*, 1976

D. HEY: *An English Rural Community*, 1974

K. S. INGLIS: *The Churches and the Working Classes in Victorian England*, 1963

A. MACFARLANE: *Witchcraft in Tudor and Stuart England*, 1970

A. MACFARLANE: *The Diary of Ralph Josselin, 1616–1683*, 1976

J. R. H. MOORMAN: *History of the Church in England*, 1967

J. R. H. MOORMAN: *Church Life in England in the Thirteenth Century*, 1946

Select Bibliography

N. ORME: *English Schools in the Middle Ages*, 1973
D. OWEN: *Church and Society in Medieval Lincolnshire*, 1971
L. F. SALZMAN: *Documentary History of Building in England*, 1952
W. E. TATE: *The Parish Chest*, 1960
K. THOMAS: *Religion and the Decline of Magic*, 1971
A. TINDALL HART: *The Country Clergy*, 1958
A. TINDALL HART: *The Man in the Pew, 1558–1660*, 1966

Index

Individual churches are indexed under the name of the town or village where they are situated. The references under the heading 'Churches' relate only to information on churches in general.